He once sold insurance –

'We found maimed is a very powerful word.
There's something horrible about being
maimed. The trouble is it's so permanent . . .'

Now he's a star of stage –

'Even by Sago's standard I was truly awful –
although some people say it was the finest
performance I have ever given . . .'

And television –

'Then you begin to realize the amazing
number of drunks in the business. People on
television are, in fact, just rather famous
drunks . . .'

He has sampled
the mystery of the orient –

'Don't point at the dog! Ignore the dog . . .'

And he has a very
attractive right leg –

'GET 'IM OFF ME!!!'

Sweet and Sour Labrador

Jasper Carrott

Text illustrations by David English

ARROW BOOKS

Arrow Books Limited
17–21 Conway Street, London W1P 6JD

An imprint of the Hutchinson Publishing Group

London Melbourne Sydney Auckland
Johannesburg and agencies throughout
the world

First published 1982

Set in Linotron Baskerville by
Rowland Phototypesetting Ltd,
Bury St Edmunds, Suffolk.

Made and printed in Great Britain
by The Anchor Press Ltd
Tiptree, Essex

ISBN 0 09 930090 7

Contents

5

Introduction

January 1980

Carrott: Another book? Already?

Publisher: Yes, well – we are doing rather well with your first book and we thought another slice of Carrott would be rather fun.

Carrott: Fun? Did you say fun?

Publisher: Well, all right – quite fun. And we would of course be prepared to pay –

£CHING!

Carrott: I'll do it. . . .

March 1981

Carrott: Now what?

Publisher: We were rather wondering how the jolly old book was coming along.

Carrott: Good question. It's now at a very critical stage of development. What we in the business call 'concept stage'.

Publisher: You mean you haven't actually written anything yet?

Carrott: Not actually written precise, solid words on the paper as yet. But the concept is *very* exciting.

Publisher: You realize, of course, that the longer the gap between your first book and the second, the greater the risk of reduced –

£CHING!

Carrott: I'll do it. . . .

November 1981

Publisher: John, Jasper's phone appears to be off the hook.

Carrott's manager: Yes, he's been getting a lot of nuisance calls recently. A *lot* of nuisance calls.

Publisher: Well, frankly John, we at HQ are all getting a bit edgy about the book.

Carrott's manager: It's at a very critical stage now.

Publisher: It's been at a critical stage for the last eleven months.

Carrott's manager: No, but I did see Jasper actually writing something the other day.

Publisher: I got that postcard. It read, 'Typewriter jammed with playdoh. Don't hold breath for book.' Now listen, John, there's quite serious talk round here of cancelling the contract and of asking you to return –

£CHING!

Carrott's manager: He'll do it. . . .

March 1982

Publisher: Jasper, I thought you'd like to know that we have now ordered the paper for your book. We have a cover and a blurb. We've taken orders from our major customers, planned the launch party, sold serialization rights, booked advertising, fixed up signing sessions –

Carrott: Great, great. It's good to hear you're on top of the job at last.

Publisher: Jasper?

Carrott: Hmmm?

Publisher: Jasper, we don't have a book – no words, nothing! And they're all waiting out there with their money in their hands, desperate to –

£CHING! £CHING!

Carrott: ALL RIGHT! I'LL DO IT!!!

That you're reading this book at all is largely due to Terence Blacker who, by ruthless application of tape recorder, typewriter and other instruments of the inquisition, proved that the age-old publishing skills of bullying, bribery and sadism towards authors still live on.

Jasper Carrott
June 1982

1 Nasty Habits

Playing with your Rubics

The Australians have an expression, 'the technicolour yawn'. Somehow that seems the perfect description for the Rubic cube.

The only people that can do the Rubic cube are kids and loonies. Kids take an average seven-and-a-half minutes, loonies fifteen seconds. There's something about that cube that defies logical explanation and, since loonies don't think logically, I suppose that's why they are so successful at it.

My record is just under thirty-four minutes, and doing it in this time is quite simple – provided you go about it logically.

The technique I'd recommend is to peel off the white stickers first – you can put the white ones on a dark surface which somehow makes them easier to find. It is absolutely essential that you heat the cube slightly, so that the stickers are easy to peel off and also to replace. The expert will notice tell-tale wrinkles so beware of the wrinkle when you are putting them back.

One of the most serious side-effects of the Rubic cube is the uncle who has mastered it, or the next-door neighbour, or the 'I can do it in seven-and-a-half minutes/ I can do it in five-and-a-half' smart-arse. And you can bet your life they've all got a quartz watch to time it. Quartz watches and Rubic cubes always go together.

Since I've personally never had time for either of them, I've worked out the only way to put the pain in the cube down.

You buy two Rubic cubes, take the blue sticker off one and the yellow sticker off the other and swap them over. You now have two cubes, one with ten blue squares and one with ten yellow squares, one of which you give to the next smart-arse who claims he can do it in five-and-a-half minutes.

My smart-arse uncle, who thinks he's really ace with the cube, now needs timing with a calendar – he's absolutely convinced that the world's against him. But the nurse says he is making excellent progress.

There are also some other unfortunate side-effects of the cube that it is wise to be aware of.

Firstly, there's 'Rubic squint'. This is caused by staring at the cube in the semi-twilight, trying to determine what the top side face edged blue is now doing on the bottom right corner 'F'. Then there's 'Rubic wrist', which is caused by manic excessive turning throughout the day and night.

Finally, if you suffer from any of these symptoms, be very careful when you're in company. For example, if you happen to arrive at the office one morning, vigorously rubbing at your wrist, complaining of its stiffness and squinting boggle-eyed at the office secretary, it is definitely a mistake to answer the knowing looks and the question 'What have you been up to?' with the answer, 'I've been playing with me rubics.'

Danger— insurance man at work!

As soon as you start work, you find you come into contact with insurance agents.

They start coming around to your house, bringing with them pictures of people mutilated in car accidents, of burning houses and of haggard old women who have been left on their own for fifteen years. After a while, they've given you this terrible guilty conscience. If I pop off, you begin to think, my poor old mum's going to have to pay for my coffin.

So they sign you up and it's only then that you begin to realize – once you're into insurance, it never stops.

As soon as an insurance man has convinced you that you ought to insure your life, then he starts to give the idea that perhaps you should also insure your mum's life – or else *you'll* have to pay for *her* coffin. Then there's your brother and your aunt and your next-door neighbour and the cat and the dog and the car and the house – just about everything you buy, you have to insure. There's just no escape.

Even if you sell something, because you can't afford to pay all this insurance, then you still have to insure it just in case the buyer sues you for the effect your sale has had on his life.

I'm now very careful about it. Once they think you have a few bob, they won't leave you alone. I've known insurance men who, seeing me drive by in the car, have turned their car around and followed me all the way home. At first, I thought I was being followed by the taxman or the law so I belted into my drive – only to see a pin-stripe clone leap out and attack me with an insurance form.

They're very persistent, insurance agents. No matter how careful you are, it's no good – they'll get you in the end. It's because they never ever take 'no' for an answer.

I'm now insured against cancer of the lower left earlobe, Legionnaire's disease, Armageddon hitting the midlands – and, of course against an insurance agent running me down in his eagerness to get me to sign one of his forms.

I was once an insurance agent for a firm with a name like the Amicable and Social – in fact, they were neither amicable nor social but they did give me a job when I feigned a lifelong, desperate craving to sell insurance. They were impressed by that.

I had already failed dismally as a barrow-boy because I had been unable to get up in the morning. Market salesmen have to get up when most people are going to bed and I found that, by the time I got to the markets, the other traders were just packing up to go.

So I got this door-knocking job for Amicable and Social, mainly because it was an evening job that fitted in with my sleep pattern.

It was simple enough really. They wanted me to sell fire and accident insurance. The hook was that fire insurance only cost ninepence a week – *very* reasonable, of course. Unfortunately, you only needed to read the actual policy to see that, even if you had a fire of Hiroshima proportions, there was little chance of repayment.

The rule was: never let them read the policy. Just scare the crap out of them.

I picked up the technique pretty quickly. Whoever answered the door, you would immediately bombard with threats of tenth degree burns and worse.

'Is this house fire protected?' you'd enquire casually. 'Looks like a lot of dry wood to me, very vulnerable. Yeah, go up in minutes, this lot. Your children will be like a load of little Guy Fawkes. Nasty, eh? Oh, by the way, are you insured against being maimed?'

We found that 'maimed' is a very powerful word. There's something horrible about being maimed. The trouble is it's so permanent. A broken leg you can live with but if you've got a *maimed* leg, you can't have a proper leg again. Ever.

So when a young housewife came to the door, you'd talk to her about raging fires in her home and permanent maiming – you just had to keep pushing that maiming bit.

Having shocked the customer into paying attention like this, some of the salesmen used to go to great lengths to make their point. They would take blow-torches into the house and big plastic buckets. Then they would put the blow-torch in the bucket.

As red-hot plastic dripped on to the carpet, they'd say, 'This could be your face, you know. Are you insured against this?'

You could calm them down at this point by asking them if they knew you could be insured against fire for as little as ninepence a week. And if you doubled it to one-and-six a week, that would insure you against being maimed.

But this was one of those policies where you were insured for loss of limb or one eye. If you happened to lose both eyes or both limbs then the policy was unfortunately null and void. There was one paragraph which said that it was not valid if the accident took place outside the house and then somewhere else on the form was another clause that stated that, if the event took place indoors, then the policy was – null and void. It was all very carefully worded.

The idea behind selling fire and personal accident insurance quite cheaply was, in fact, a very cunning ploy. It meant that the collector would call every week to collect the ninepence and, of course, he would have direct access to the family. He would have been calling for about a month when he would come in with the big heavies – life insurance, death insurance, the lot. He really had you then.

I was never really very successful at selling insurance. I'd go in and try to sell something but they would always manage to sell me something first like a raffle ticket or a ticket to the local amateur dramatic society. So I'd come out in the red.

In the end, I had to leave because I wasn't doing the figures. I spent too much time in the evening attending all the social functions I'd bought tickets for.

I think I had only managed to sell one real fire policy – it was 3b Watery Street, Bordesley. Three months after I left Amicable and Social I was driving down Watery Street and there was 3b – burnt to the ground.

On balance my career as an insurance agent must have lost them around £8000.

Now I'm on the receiving end, it's completely different.

Quite recently I asked a man from an insurance company to come round because I was looking for some kind of family security and I knew that this particular firm had a good policy.

A bloke came round with a little case within about two days of my call and, although he didn't have to sell me anything because I knew what I wanted anyway, he insisted on opening up his little case. Inside was a small projector and screen with a sound apparatus which he set up.

He sat my wife and I down and made us sit through a film showing all the misery and gloom in the world and just what his firm could do about it – all couched in terms that suggested that they were doing you a favour.

Unfortunately for him we were having some building work done in the house at the time so suddenly in the middle of this subtle soft sell, an electric drill and pump hammer would drown everything out. So our man would lean surreptitiously over and turn the volume full blast. It would just about be holding its own against the noise – 'We will take care of your family in the event of personal tragedy, accident . . .' – when the electric drill would stop, leaving only the film show at full volume – 'AND OF SERIOUS, IRREPARABLE MAIMING OF LIMBS.'

He'd have to dive across to turn it down until the noise outside started up again. Then up he'd pop to turn it up, then to turn it down again. Up and down, up and down – it was like listening to the World Service when the reception's bad.

But insurance companies train their men to be ready for all eventualities so this man was not in the least put out by all this. On the other hand, the fact that I knew exactly the policy I wanted threw him completely. He was so fully trained that, even when I'd signed the papers, he was still selling me what I'd already bought because he just couldn't stop the patter.

In the end, after we had signed up and given him the money, I started making some tea and my wife was clearing some things up while he was still following us around the house showing us photos of maimed children and funeral processions.

As we closed the door on him, he was still talking – I think he was just about getting to halfway through his programmed sales pitch.

Picking up girls

I've never been any good at chatting up girls.

'I've discovered it's something you can either do or you can't – and, if you can't, you're always meeting the blokes that can.

Some of my friends are fantastic – they never fail. One of them will walk into a bar, stroll up to a girl. 'Hullo there,' he says. 'What are you doing here?'

The girl will go weak at the knees and giggle.

'Waiting for someone like you.'

I tried that approach.

'Hullo there,' I said. 'What are *you* doing here?'

'Avoiding creeps like you.'

But I kept trying. A friend gave me a book called *How to Score at a Party*, and I learnt that basically what you have to do is go round and grin at everybody. Eventually you've got to get lucky.

So I went to this party and grinned solidly for four hours.

'Hi, there . . . hello there . . . what are you –'

Not a light. Total failure.

I went home that night and, when I looked in the bathroom mirror, I saw I'd got this great piece of green cabbage stuck between my front teeth. I'd been walking around all evening with it.

'Hi, there . . . hello there.'
'What's 'e got between 'is teeth, Beryl?'
'Looks like a piece of spinach to me.'
'No, it's too green for that.'
'Mmm, I don't know. Maybe 'is nose is running . . .'

2 Bazza Carrott

Australian sticky tape

Flying to Australia is one of the ultimate tests of endurance. It takes over twenty-four hours and you never ever manage to take enough to read. You could take *The Lord of the Rings* and a complete set of the *Encyclopaedia Britannica* and you'd still be reading the back of matchboxes by the end of the trip.

The last time I made the journey, I started reading one of these motor sport magazines and I just happened to come across this full-page photograph of a Formula One racing car which was sponsored by Durex. So there it was – this beautiful, sleek racing car with Durex written all over it – and it's in the pits with a burst tyre.

Funny but worrying, I thought.

I ripped this photo out of the magazine and, when I got to Australia, I started showing all the Aussies the Durex car with the burst tyre.

There wasn't even a titter. Not a glimmer of a giggle. A total sense of humour failure.

It was then that I found out that, believe it or not, Durex is on sale in Australia, but it is in fact the brand name of the best-selling sticky tape. We have Sellotape – they have Durex. Very confusing – it caught me out a couple of times.

When you go into a chemist in this country, it's all very low-key and embarrassed. You look round furtively, see if the coast is clear, walk up to the assistant and ask boldy, 'Um, yes, oh crikey, er . . . serve the lady first . . . Um, a packet of, er, drrrmmbble, please.'

'Yer what?'

'A bottle of Lucozade.'

But in department stores in Australia, big Aussies would come in and shout, 'Gooday! A packet of Durex there – giant size.' And they'd give them a big roll of sticky tape. Well, I thought, I've heard of do-it-yourself . . . .

I've been meaning to do this in London. I'll go to Earl's Court, where all the Australians stay when they come over here, and pay a few visits to stationers there because the reverse has just got to happen, hasn't it?

Some fresh-faced Australian is going to come in and he won't know.

'A roll of Durex, please,' he'll bawl at the assistant.

And the assistant will be thinking, 'A roll? A *roll* of Durex? I'd love to see his Christmas presents.'

Yokel radio

The media in Australia are run on a completely different basis from over here. Because it is such a vast continent, news all tends to come from local television and radio rather than a national network.

My very first local radio interview in Australia was on a station in Melbourne called 2CR. It was run by public donation and had a total staff of about four.

The interview was in a very small room decorated in hessian – it was a bit like doing an interview in a sack – and was being conducted by a bloke from Smallheath, Birmingham.

I've found that, wherever you go in the world, there will be someone there who comes from Smallheath and he'll find you. On this occasion he ran the radio station.

It was all very friendly and relaxed. We chatted on the air about home and generally behaved as if what we were saying had nothing to do with radio or the public at all. People were walking in and out of the studio and interrupting us with questions like, 'Will you be home tonight, Robert?' And he'd say 'Yes' and go on with the interview as they left, saying, 'Fine, I'll leave the key under the mat.'

I was sitting mesmerized as all this went on. One part of the interview went:

'Would you like a cup of tea?'

'Er, yes. That would be nice.'

'Milk? One sugar?'

'Yes, please.'

'Now where's that sugar gone?'

And you'd hear all this banging and knocking as he got the tea together. Then we'd go on with the interview.

'Here you go. Is that enough sugar?'

'Yes, fine.'

'Right, why don't we put it down over here away from all these papers?'

I wondered who on earth was listening to this drivel.

He was fairly left-wing this bloke – in fact, he made Jane Fonda look like Norman Tebbit. So, when we did finally get away from talking about the tea, he wanted to turn anything I said into a political discussion of some sort.

He really needed to know where I stood on feminism, chauvinism, gay liberation, conservation, the need for creche facilities on whaling ships – that sort of thing.

There was also a woman in the room who happened to pick up the fact that I was a director of Birmingham City – as soon as she heard that, her attitude towards me changed. She was obviously convinced that I was secretly a capitalist bed-wetter and was more than a little disappointed when I told her that football directors don't earn anything – in fact, they actually put money in. She had no answer to that so the discussion shifted on to why there were no women professional footballers in Britain. Do you know, I couldn't answer that one.

In Sydney, I had one of the most esoteric interviews I have ever experienced. The interviewer was an ex-patriot folk music enthusiast, and he insisted on talking for about an hour on this major radio station about the people I used to play with. It was strange sitting there in an Australian studio, calmly discussing Tony Capstick and Noel Murphy and swopping gossip about the British folk club scene.

This guy later told me how he took great delight in asking Australians if it had cost their parents £10 to get there or whether they had got their passage free.

There's no quicker way to upset people in Australia than to mention convicts . . . The one thing you must never bring up in conversation out there is anklets – they don't like it at all.

Australian (no) Rules Football

Australians are very passionate about an extremely strange sport called Australian Rules Football.

I never quite mastered the way the game works. It is played on a pitch that is basically circular so there's absolutely no way of telling which way each team is meant to be playing.

In fact, the only thing that I can remember about the game is that virtually anything goes. It's a misleading name, Australian Rules Football, because there are no rules.

For a start, you can do anything with the ball: kick it, throw it, pick it up and run like hell with it. You can do the same things with the opposing players as well.

It's a bit rough, there's no denying it. The players pride themselves on their macho – few prisoners are taken. They have even made all the football shirts sleeveless to stop the players ripping them off and strangling the opposition with them.

One of the things that I could never for the life of me understand was why, when the game is going at full tilt, everyone suddenly stops and stands looking at the guy who has just caught the ball. He is then allowed all the time in the world to score a goal from where he stands. Most odd.

Finally they end up with these massive scores – something like 735–490.

Although there appear to be no rules, they do have at least fifteen referees there to administer them.

While I was in Australia, a very big game took place between two local sides which ended up on the front page of the newspapers. There had been a great furore at the end of the game because the referee – or one of the fifteen referees – had failed to hear the siren that goes off inside the ground to mark the end of the match. He blew his whistle after a three-or four-second delay and, of course, in those seconds one of the teams scored the winning goal.

It was a national scandal. The referee was banished – there was serious talk of sending him back to England in anklets and handcuffs.

Somebody suggested that in future an electric pulse should be fitted to the referee's heart so that, when the siren went, someone at siren headquarters could throw a switch that would electrocute the referee on the spot.

They thought that would finish the game in a tidy, uncontroversial way.

Death in Canberra

The difficulty a performer has in Australia is in its size. You can be very popular in one part of the country and completely unknown in another. I played to very good audiences in most of the big towns – Melbourne, Adelaide, Sydney, Perth and Brisbane – but I died the death in Canberra.

I was playing at a 1200 seater. They sold 125 tickets. In fact, I'm still not sure who those were sold to since absolutely no one had heard of me in Canberra, having done no television or newspaper interviews there at all.

Looking back on it, I've come to the conclusion that the reason I sold those tickets was that *anything* beats walking round Canberra, which has to be the most boring capital in the world. This is strange, since I honestly rated the country as a whole one of the best I've been to, and the people some of the most interesting I've met.

Everything in Canberra has been built with mind-numbing logic, so that it is all in tidy blocks and squares. All the car showrooms are on one block, the television shops on the next, record shops on the next and so on. Totally organised and mechanical, it's the most characterless place I have ever visited.

Someone told me the suicide rate per capita in Canberra is one of the highest in the world. I nearly added to that statistic.

So those 125 people were clearly there to fight off the boredom. They'd never heard of me but, even if I was the worst comic on earth, I just had to be more interesting than Canberra.

The theatre itself was typically Canberraian – symmetrical, square and functional.

I remember little about that night except my first sound check. As I went out on to the stage, I looked out into the auditorium and saw that all the seats were covered in pure white vinyl. It was like a block of tombstones staring you in the face.

Wonderful, I thought, there's going to be more than 1000 of these tombstones staring at me tonight – fantastic for atmosphere. Everybody in the room would be aware of just how badly I'd done and even the 125 who had gambled on a ticket would be thinking that this would be a loser. They'd probably all go out and commit suicide after the show.

'Blimey,' I said to the stage doorman standing by, 'the seats look just like the tombstones.'

'Yup,' he said. 'One for every artist who's died here. They're just fixing yours in right now.'

3 He'll Never Learn

French 'O' Level

One of my best subjects at school was French. I did in fact pass my mock 'O' Level in French – I got 17 per cent. I was top of the class, too.

I think I failed my GCE proper because of inadequate teaching, although they did give me special tuition in French for about six months after I got this 17 per cent.

Unfortunately, it never really worked. This teacher I had was really a bit weird. He kept giving me these very odd French books to read – I think I'd appreciate them now, but at the time I was most confused.

He never taught me the rudiments of exams and when the day came for me to take my GCE, it all came as a bit of a shock to me. For one thing, they split me up from my mate – that was half the knowledge gone for a start.

Then the teacher at the front gave out these brown paper envelopes which you're not allowed to open until he gives the word. When we'd all got our envelopes, he just said '*Allez*' and everyone started getting their papers out – all except me because I hadn't a clue what he was on about. I thought that they were all cheating.

Eventually, I thought that I had better cheat as well so I got my papers out of the envelope and, would you believe it, they were all in French!

How unlucky can you get, I thought. My counterpart in Paris has the English papers.

So I went up to the bloke at the front and asked him to translate it. He got really snotty. If I hadn't been reading all these strange books, I wouldn't have understood a word he said. Nobody else knew what he was going on about, but I had a fairly good idea.

So I went back to my seat and wrote out thirty-two verses of the French Eskimo Nell, which was my party piece at the time, and I ended up getting 17 per cent again.

So someone had a sense of humour anyway. . . .

What am I bid?

If I inherited anything from my father, it was his mania for buying cheap, second-hand, completely useless bargains.

He used to buy the most ridiculous things. One of my early childhood memories is of the day he bought 5000 used street lamp covers from Birmingham City Council and stored them in the garden. What he ever thought he was going to do with these covers, no one ever found out because he always lost interest in things once he had bought them. Of course, my friends and I had a great time lugging bricks at them so that, after a while, our garden was just like a glass tip.

Because of this compulsion of my father's, we had a front room that was almost impossible to get into. He was an electrician and used the front room to store all kinds of electrical junk. He was renowned throughout the trade for his habit of hoarding obscure and outdated bits of electrical gubbins.

We'd get loads of visits from people looking for parts for their old pre-war radios – my dad would let them loose to ferret about for themselves. I'd find complete strangers in our front room searching for an SF1038 valve.

One of my dad's most serious addictions was to auctions – he just couldn't resist them – and, for a while, it looked as if I was going to have the same problem.

My favourite haunt was an auction house in Birmingham. The auctioneer there was an unforgettable character. He had very little patience with people – not exactly an advantage in his position.

His general manner was not unlike Basil Fawlty's – only not quite so charming.

You could never tell how he was going to be. On a good day, if the auction was going reasonably well, he'd be smiling and really quite decent to people. But he hated pitherers. People who pithered were made to feel decidedly unwelcome.

If he felt he was being messed around – an article that he felt was worth £50 was attracting bids of £15, for example, then he'd turn nasty. He'd start out quietly cynical, then he'd become scathing and finally contemptuous.

'Oh, we have got the crème de la crème in today, my word,' he'd say. 'And are the Vanderbilts present today? How about the Rockefellers? Ah good – they're here too.

'Now we have this wonderful reproduction Dali that, with such a wealth of sophisticated, well-educated intellectuals, will have absolutely no problem in reaching the reserve and well beyond.

'What am I bid? Ah, five pound fifty from Mrs Vanderbilt at the back. What a wonderful generous bid. Remember this is by Salvador Dali – that's spelt D – A – L – I. Now, come on Rockefellers – you're not going to let the Vanderbilts get away with this, are you? Oh, six-fifty, I hear. That's what I like to see – throwing caution to the wind.

'Frank,' he'd say, turning to his assistant, 'there's no use letting anyone else in. Both the Vanderbilts *and* the Rockefellers are here – they'll outbid everybody. Better clear a space for their fleet of Securicor vans at the back.'

Not surprisingly, this monologue made people a little nervous, particularly when he reacted to an opening bid of which he disapproved with a contemptuous 'tut' – as if words couldn't express his despair for a human who could make such a humiliating bid.

Then he'd just turn on someone in his audience. 'Hey you!' he'd say. 'Have you bid this morning? Well, if you haven't bid, what are you standing around here for? Waiting for a bus? We don't sell buses here – try the corporation. All right – why haven't you bid?'

'Well, there's nothing I've wanted.'

'Nothing you've wanted! What d'you mean, nothing you've wanted? We've had forty paintings through. Surely *something's* taken your fancy?'

'Actually, I'm waiting for lot 301.'

'Oh, he's waiting for lot 301. We have a real connoisseur here. He's interested in lot 301. Right, we'll skip the next seventy so that our friend the spy from Sothebys doesn't have to endure them before he gets to his lot 301. Pull out lot 301, Frank. Now, what am I bid?'

'Twenty-five pounds?

'Twenty-five pounds? Did you say? You've got no chance. You've been waiting here all morning, wasting my time, everyone's time and then you bid – Can I at least have a sensible bid? Twenty-nine? Ridiculous. Frank take it away. He'll just have to wait until a bus comes.'

On another occasion, he was asking for bids for a washing machine and the bidding had slowly edged up to around £7 when a bloke at the back piped up, 'Does it work?'

The auctioneer looked at the man incredulously. 'Does it *matter*?'

'Yes, I'll bid more if it works.'

'Well, it must have worked once,' he said. 'Isn't that enough?'

And without further ado, he slammed his hammer down. 'Sold for seven-fifty to me. That'll teach you not to pither!'

4 Right Leg Fever

Right Leg Fever

I've mentioned before now one of my most serious afflictions – I am cursed with a right leg that arouses the desire of any male dog that happens to be passing.

I used to think that this only happened to me, but I've now discovered that many people have the same problem. They have a *femme fatale* limb.

One bloke actually admitted that he had a head that tended to be the object of amorous attention from butchers' dogs. I dread to think of it!

It's difficult to remember when I first became aware of this particularly embarrassing problem. When I was young, I put it down to the fact that animals just adored me but, as I grew older, I came to realize that it was something a little more serious.

Of course, there's not a lot that you can do about it. You can't exactly go along to the doctor, inform him that your leg is constantly being raped, and ask him for a deterrent pill on the National Health.

I tried that powder they spray around bitches' bums when they're in season. Well, it did work – dogs flung themselves under buses and stuck their tails in light sockets rather than be around that smell – but you tended to get the most peculiar looks at social gatherings, particularly from members of the RSPCA. So, after a while, I realized that it was just something you have to put up with.

I finally came to terms with the seriousness of my

problem when I had a job delivering groceries in and around the wealthy borough of Solihull.

Now, delivering groceries to houses protected by watchdogs with a right leg guaranteed to give an airedale a multiple orgasm is not a job approved by the Trades Safety Council.

For a start, you are fairly defenceless as you stagger up the garden, loaded with a cornflake carton brimming over with the weekly shopping. I became very adept at ringing the bell with my nose.

'Good morning, madam. Your groceries from EEEYAHHHH!'

There would follow a short act from Sadler's Wells as I hopped around the garden trying to shake free a corgi that was hanging on for dear life.

'GET THIS DAMN DOG OFF ME!'

'It's all right. He won't be long!'

Every order used to have scrambled egg in it.

But it was worth putting up with these minor tribulations of the job just for the sheer joy of driving a lorry. A much maligned occupation, in my opinion, and very underrated as a pastime.

There's something very macho about lorry driving. As you bowl along, you have plenty of time to fantasize about being a tank commander – or even Rommel going into action against the desert rats.

I first got into truck driving while working on a holiday camp. Immediately seeing my potential, they sent me to a truck-driving school. It was there that I fell in love with the great multi-wheeled beasts.

You soon learn that there is a very strict code of conduct in truck driving. Every driver must have the utmost consideration for other truckers. The macho image must be upheld at all costs.

The first lesson you learn at the school is how to letch out of the cab window. Every time you pass a young lady in the street, you have to hang bodily out of the cab window and gesticulate with your right arm clasped firmly in the crook by your left hand. Then, with the regulation leer, you accompany the gesture with something like, 'Fancy you a bit, darlin',' or 'Where d'ya get them legs!'

The young ladies in general react in the same way: you get the disdainful look, the flick of the hair, the contemptuous look of studied indifference.

But if you *don't* letch and leer, my word, do you get some stick!

'Hey, what's the matter with me, you . . . you . . . you *homosexual*!'

Having passed through the lorry school, all I ever wanted to do was drive a lorry. Hence the job with the groceries.

One particular advantage to this job was that I could nick the lorries in the evenings to go to discos and dances. I'd rumble into the car park in this three-tonner, generally leaving it in the middle of the park so that inferior machines couldn't get past.

Once you were in the club or dance hall, of course, no one would know what you were driving so you could be really cool.

'Hey! Hi there! I'm a computer programmer. I have my own personalized digital pen.'

'Gosh! Oh, really! Wow!'

I used to chat up the girls and offer them a lift home – without actually mentioning what they were going home in.

46

When they saw the truck, they could hardly believe their eyes – particularly when they saw the height of the cab and realized the rope and tackle job that was needed to get them up there. It was the age of the mini-skirt and I have to admit that the odd peek – all right, stare – added to my enjoyment of the occasion.

Unfortunately, my success rate with the lorry was not great. In fact, my friendship with them used to last until the moment when we arrived at their front door.

Now you can't be suave in a three-tonner, so you get to the point.

'Any chance of seeing you again?'

'Get lost, creep!'

'Good night, then.'

'Good night!' they'd say, stepping out into the void. 'EEEYAAAHHHHHRRRGGG!'

'Mind the step.'

One night I went off in my lorry to a really posh dance in Solihull. All the hooray Henrys in the neighbourhood were there, walking around competing as to whose chin was receding the fastest.

I was looking particularly smooth that night. I had my white suit on and a pair of dark glasses. It would have looked terrific – trouble was, I'd trodden on the glasses earlier in the evening so I was standing on the side of the dance floor looking at 5000 dancers through my fractured lenses.

At one stage of the evening, I found myself next to this very posh young lady. Her name was Davina Jacobson.

'Hi there, Davina! Hey, I'm a computer programmer. I have my own personalized digital pen.'

'Gosh, really?'

It never failed.

After a while I asked her if she wanted a lift home.

'Well, I really don't know, Jaspah,' she said. 'I was going home with Malcolm but Malcolm's gorn orf with Henry.'

'Don't worry, Dav,' I said. 'I've got some wheels.'

'Really?'

'Yeah. Eight of 'em.'

So she said it was absolutely super and, a little later, I suggested we headed off home.

When we got out to the car park, she took one look at the lorry and shrieked.

'*Fabuloso!*'

'Eh?'

'It's a *lorry*! I've never been in a lorry before. Is it yours, Jaspah?'

'Mmm, er, yes.'

'Oh, yippee! I'm going home in a lorry!'

Hullo, I thought, this is going to be interesting.

She was obviously into equestrian sports because she leapt straight into the cab. Driving home, she was ecstatic.

'What a fabulous lorry, Jaspah! Look at all those Yorkies. And that scrummy bacon – I just love bacon!'

I was convinced that I had absolutely no chance here, but when I went into my 'See you again?' routine, she was as keen as anything.

'Oh, rather,' she said. 'Come round tomorrow – it's Sunday. We'll go for a spin in the truck. Call round after dinner – and don't forget to bring the bacon!'

At that stage, I thought anything was worth a try, so the next morning it was shave, shower, and out with the bacon joint for a quick rub under the arms and off I went.

Davina's house had a big gravel drive so I burnt round there three or four times kicking up the gravel before pulling up outside the front door. Leaving the drive looking like a Wimpey site, I walked up to the door and rang the bell with my nose – somehow I just couldn't kick the habit.

Davina's mother came to the door. She took one look at me and said, 'No, thank you, we're Sainsbury's.'

'No,' I said. 'I'm here for Davina.'

'Are you Jaspah?'

'Yes.'

'Oh dear,' she said and shouted into the house, 'Davina, it's Jaspah!'

Davina quickly appeared.

'Oh, fabuloso! Yippee, Mummy, he's got a super big lorry with eight wheels. Isn't he absolutely sweet? Mummy, this is Jaspah. Jaspah . . . Mummy.'

I was just going 'How do you do, Mrs Jacobson. Very pleased to meet –' when, at that precise moment, Sebastian arrives.

Sebastian was their Afghan and he gave me no chance. He spotted that right leg and suddenly it was Sadler's Wells again.

'*Get 'im off me!*' I was yelling as they were beating him with bricks, sticks and anything that came to hand.

'Kick his balls!' Mrs Jacobson shouted.

That was all I needed. By leaping three yards in the air, I could screw my left foot round and deliver a

Trevor Francis special – right between Sebastian's thrusting legs.

'No!' she screamed. 'His balls! The ones on the lawn!'

But by that time there were tears in my eyes, never mind Sebastian's.

Eventually I was taken into the lounge to meet Davina's father. He wasn't too impressed.

'You look a mess,' he said.

'I should think so. I've just been raped by your Afghan.'

The whole family was there so I had to go around the room meeting aunties, uncles, grannies, brothers, sisters – the whole Jacobson hunting set. They didn't take too much notice of me as everyone was wondering where the hell the smell of bacon was coming from. After a while, I stood behind a plant with my arms rigidly by my side.

I was thinking, 'I bet they're Jewish. I *bet* they're Jewish.'

About an hour later, they brought in tea and cucumber sandwiches. While we were all chatting away, Sebastian appeared, limping slightly.

Luckily, he was too knackered by now to pay me any attention. Instead, he sat down in the middle of the room and started methodically licking his bum.

Now isn't that embarrassing? I mean, where do you look? No one's going to say anything, are they? They're not going to say, 'Stop licking your arsehole, Sebastian.'

In desperation, to break the acute embarrassment of the occasion, I said, 'Cor, I wish I could do that.'

It was just to break the ice – crack a little funny, that sort of thing.

But you always know when you've said the wrong

50

thing. People start spluttering and coughing and fingering their collars.

Thankfully, it was Davina's mum who let me off the hook. She looked me in the eye and smiled sweetly.

'If you give him a biscuit, he'll let you.'

5 Comics' Lib

Comics' Lib

Not many people realize that, if things carry on as they are, by the beginning of the twenty-first century there will be no comedy.

By then, laughter will be a bit like smoking is now; socially unacceptable, definitely anti-Christian and a clear sign of a low degree of intelligence. Like cigarettes, jokes will be progressively banned from restaurants, theatres and other public places so that eventually it will only be possible to indulge in a good laugh furtively in attics, cellars and secret underground clubs.

It all dates back to the socially responsible seventies. This was when we all began to realize that, because the natural trigger for all laughter is a sense of superiority to the object of the humour, you are therefore laughing at the unfortunate, the deprived, the underdogs.

So that was the end of any joke that was based on the idea that one race was different from another – all that was classed as racialist. Any sketches that portrayed the Germans as being a little cold, the Spaniards as being vaguely excitable or the French as being a trifle arrogant were definitely *out*.

Of course, this now means that we are witnessing the death throes of the Englishman, Scotsman, Welshman, Irishman joke as we know it. The basic assumptions are having to change.

Instead of the Englishman being stiff upper-lipped, the Scotsman being mean, the Welshman singing all the time and the Irishman being ignorant, we are having to change the emphasis a bit. The Scotsman, for example, has to be a diligent, well-dressed Highlander who is generous to a fault. The Welshman will probably be a socially aware, anti-nuclear environmentalist and the Irishman will be well-educated and an expert on the works of Aristophanes.

If anyone is mean, stupid, tone-deaf and ignorant, I'm afraid it's going to have to be the Englishman.

The big question for comics is whether the Englishman, Scotsman etc. joke is going to survive this new age of moral awareness. And how will we know if our jokes are pure enough?

I imagine that, once again, the only solution will be the Common Market. Perhaps they will set up a Eurogag Commission that will carefully inspect any new jokes that come up and make suggested changes.

What, for example, would this futuristic Eurogag Commission suggest a comic does with the old, highly nationalistic joke concerning three United Kingdom citizens:

An Englishman, an Irishman and a Scotsman were sitting in a pub and asked the barman for some drinks.

The Irishman ordered a round: a gin and tonic for the Englishman, a Guinness for himself and a Horlicks for the Scotsman.

The Englishman ordered a round: a Guinness for the Irishman, a gin and tonic for himself and a Horlicks for the Scotsman.

When it came to the Scotsman's turn to buy a round, he was fast asleep.

1) The basic nationalistic premise of the joke needs to be rethought now that distinct nationalities within the EEC are no longer acceptable. Therefore, replace the principal characters in the joke so that the Englishman, Irishman and Scotsman are now all Europeople.

2) The setting of the joke poses a problem. The three Euro-people are 'sitting in a pub' and this is clearly an occupation with distinct chauvinistic overtones. The setting should be at the very minimum a refreshment lounge or preferably a Eurocommunity centre.

3) 'Barman' is unacceptable. If crudity is essential, we will accept 'barperson' but in our view the story would be best served by reference to a 'qualified liquid stimulant operative'.

4) The fact that there is not one woman or 'Eurogay' (a Europerson of undecided sexual preference) is a clear breach of the EEC Non-Sexist Code, the assumption being that only men socialize in Eurocommunity Centres, while the other three sexes stay at home bringing up children or knitting, as the case may be. We therefore recommend that, in this joke, there should be one Euroman, one Eurowoman and two Eurogays.

5) The choice of drinks in the uncensored story is overtly objectionable. *Gin and tonic*: classist in its implications. Suggest Euroman orders half a mild with a cherry.

(Will all comics please note that all future references to a *Bloody Mary* will be severely dealt with. This drink has sexist and anti-religious undertones as well as offending the Frau Weithaus anti-violence guidelines. The actual consumption of this drink is, of course, strictly forbidden following the EEC boycott of Channel Island tomatoes, imposed as a result of the Jersey government's unauthorised showing of a Benny Hill Show on public television.)

Guinness: clearly racist. Far too black to drink. Euro-woman should drink Newcastle Brown – correction, Newcastle Dark Pigment Ale.

(Will all comics please note that all future references to cocktails will not be accepted – we refer them to item 23(b) of the Non-Sexist Code. Replace with organtails.)

Horlicks: this term has been completely banned from the EEC on the grounds of its disgusting and overt sexual implications. Frankly, in the view of this commission, it leaves a nasty taste in the mouth. Suggested alternatives would include München Draughtshlurpen, which is well known in southern Bavaria for its soporific effects.

6) When it comes to the turn of the Eurogays to buy a round, it should not be implied that they were not prepared to participate in communal responsibilities to the same degree as everyone else since this would imply laziness and inability to concentrate on the job in hand.

There would be a definite implication here that people of a non-heterosexual inclination are unwilling to contribute to the same degree and therefore would be classed as mean. This is a most disagreeable and unacceptable state of affairs.

It should not be forgotten that Eurogays are now responsible for Eurocommissioners' expenses.

The commission therefore recommends that, when it is time for the third round to be bought, the Eurogays should react in a non-demeaning manner – a simple blink would suffice.

The version authorized by the Eurogag Commission now reads as follows:

A Euroman, a Eurowoman and two Eurogays were in a Eurocommunity Centre having a drink.

The liquid stimulant operative asked them what they were having.

'A half of mild with a cherry, please,' said the Euroman.

'A Newcastle Dark Pigment Ale, please,' said the Eurowoman.

'And two München Draughtschlurpens, please,' said the Eurogays.

And the Euroman paid.

When it was time for another round, the Eurowoman asked them all what they would like.

'I'll have a half of mild with a cherry,' said the Euroman.

'Two München Draughtschlurpen for us,' said the Eurogays.

'And a Newcastle Dark Pigment Brown for me,' said the Eurowoman.

When the liquid stimulant operative came round for the third time, they ordered again.

'A half of mild with a cherry,' said the Euroman.

'A Newcastle Dark Pigment Ale,' said the Eurowoman.

The Eurogays blinked!

My only hope is that the spirit of the true Brit wit will survive through covert resistance. Secret videos of 'The Les Dawson Show' will be passed from hand to hand. Illicit laughing clubs will spring up. I'll be Hon. Sec. of Comics' Lib.

Of course, I realize the dangers. Hiding from the Eurogag Special Police who will be touring the streets in their laughter-detector vans.

I have this nightmare. One night, we'll all be sitting in an underground pub surreptitiously sipping Guinness and swopping mother-in-law jokes when they'll burst in, toting cases of Bernard Manning anti-laughter cassettes.

'*Freeze!*' they'll say. 'This is a bust. One giggle and we'll play the tapes!'

6 Carrott del Sol

Take one:
An epic is born

... There were three of us careering drunkenly through Manchester airport, spraying everyone in sight with beer, barging to the front of queues and generally behaving in a disgusting manner, hotly pursued by a complete television crew. None of the people using the airport raised one word of objection. We'd probably just covered someone's new holiday coat with warm beer and we simply said, 'It's for television.'

'Oh, right,' they said, understanding immediately. 'Right. Fine.'

... we were doing a beach scene and one of us noticed that the dark glasses I was wearing reflected what I was looking at into the camera. So we thought it would be an idea if I made a remark for the film about not worrying about birds, followed by a shot of the reflection of a topless woman in my glasses. Since we didn't have a topless woman handy, the stage production manager John Quilty went over to a girl of about nineteen who was sunbathing on the beach.

'Would you like to be in a film?' he asked.

'Yes, please,' she said.

So she came over in her bikini and Quilty added, 'Oh, and if you could take your top off, please. You're going to be topless.'

'Okay,' she said, not batting an eyelid. 'Fine, right.' And started undressing.

. . . we had all the hidden cameras set up and the three characters in the film were going to give this unsuspecting Spanish waiter a hard time.

When he came to the table, we spoke to each other in very loud voices so that he could overhear. We were saying things like, 'The louder you speak the more they understand,' and 'Put "o" on the end of everything and they'll get the gist.'

So then we ordered. 'One pint-o of Watneys Red Barrel-o, one cup of tea-o, and a Vimto-o. A Vimto-o. *Vimto-o!*'

It was all delivered in thick Brummie accents and at a speed that made it unintelligible even to the most native of Birmingham residents.

But he just said, 'No Watneys Red Barrel-o, no tea-o, no Vimto-o,' and walked off.

Somehow these three incidents sum up my memories of the making of 'Carrott del Sol'.

What I wanted to do in the film was build on a documentary that I had made in America called 'Carrott Gets Rowdy', which looked at soccer in the States. Shot very much on the run and in an ad-lib style, it was a documentary with humour.

We had gone out to America with the idea of making a documentary first and foremost but planned to inject comedy into situations as and when they happened.

For example, during the filming we came across a fast food restaurant with a drive-in facility.

Being in something of a hurry, I drove up to the drive-in section to order some drinks. Much to my amazement, you had to place your order with a talking sign! This was, in effect, a large neon board on which snacks and drinks were advertised. In the corner was a grill at which you shouted your order. No human in sight – ultimate automation!

This was a chance too good to miss. We set the cameras and sound and then I proceeded to have a conversation with the sign – chatting it up, attempting to date it and ending with the line, 'See you later. Oh, and remember – wear something casual!'

This particular sequence was without doubt the highlight of the film. People still ask me about it.

So, with the success of this scene in mind, I felt it was worth exploring further the improvisational approach to comedy film.

But in 'Carrott del Sol', we decided we would bring comedy to the fore. Keeping the freewheeling, shoot-on-the-run style that we used for the American programme, we would this time go specifically for laughs and use real people in real situations.

This way, it would have a type of candid camera approach while going one step further – you wouldn't just laugh the people who didn't know what was going on but also, we hoped, at the principal characters in the film, who were ad libbing within that framework.

We knew that comedy of this type couldn't hope to be one hundred per cent perfectly timed or constructed but we were aiming for humour on different levels – the ad libs by the main characters and the innocence of people in real situations – and hoped that the essence of the programme would make people laugh.

The two other artists in the film were Terry Molloy and Bernard Latham, both professional actors who, we hoped, could ad lib comedy within situations as they happened. I specifically avoided very well-known faces or professional comics because I simply wanted actors who would be relatively unknown – that way, there would be no preconceptions on the public's part.

We had a general story line around which we would work. We'd be three blokes going out on a typical package holiday abroad and the film would highlight what happens to them – without, we hoped, resorting to standard Spanish jokes or stereotypes.

That was the idea behind 'Carrott del Sol'. It was, to say the least, a gamble.

Much to their credit, London Weekend Television agreed to do it.

Michael Grade, then controller of LWT, must have had a minor wobbly before he finally gave his consent. After all, what had he got to go on?

'Right, Jasper. What's the next project?'

'Well, Mike, I'd like to take a film crew to the Costa del Sol in the summer and do some, er, some filming.'

'Oh, yes – what about?'

'Three yobboes on holiday.'

'Ye-es. So you'll be working with other actors?'

'Yes.'

'Interesting. Different for you, too. Who are the actors?'

'Bernard Latham and Terry Molloy.'

Michael Grade is familiar with most people in the business, but he couldn't quite recall these two particular guys.

'Terry Molloy,' he said. 'Is he, er, was he in. . . . Who is Terry Molloy?'

'Oh, you know him, Mike. He's done several of 'The Archers' episodes. I think he was a hissing bar-tap once.'

'And Bernard Latham. . . . His name does ring a faint bell.'

'Yes, Bernard did an audition for a Mars advert once.'

'Oh, yes,' said Mike, '*that* Bernard Latham. And where's the script?'

'There isn't really going to be a script.'

'No script?'

'No script.'

'Well, what's the story-line then?'

'There isn't one of those either.'

'Well. . . . How do you see the start of the film?'

'That depends on the end.'

'And the end depends on the beginning?'

Mike catches on quick.

'So let's get this right,' he says, with a look that says, 'Please don't let this sound as bad as I think it's going to sound.'

'You and two unknown actors, masquerading as three yobboes, are taking a highly trained, expensive film crew to the Costa del Sol in the summer to shoot a film that has no story, no end, no script and, if something turns up, you'll make a comedy skit out of it.'

66

'A liberal form of that, yes.'

I knew it wasn't going to be easy. In fact, I had prepared myself to deliver the ultimate in artist versus mogul persuasion. It goes something like: 'I SEE. ONCE AGAIN THE PARASITIC, CAPATALIST HIERARCHY OF THE MEDIA MONOPOLIES, HAVING SAT ON THEIR FAT ARSES, LIVING OFF THE SWEATED LABOUR EFFORTS OF HIGHLY SENSITIVE ARTISTIC TALENTS, SUPPRESS AN ADVENTUROUS, FUTURISTIC BREAKTHROUGH IN THE SURREALISTIC DEVELOPMENT OF THE PERFORMING ARTS!!!'

I put on my 'highly sensitive artistic talent' face and started, 'I SEE –'

'Okay, Carrott,' says Mike quickly. 'Just get on and do it. But don't tell anyone too much about it – I'll say you're making a documentary.'

Take two: The next flight to Bedlam

I never cease to be amazed at what people will be prepared to do when there is a film camera about. I had ample opportunity to discover this again over the next three weeks.

Ray Marshall, the producer of 'Carrott del Sol', had the unenviable task of getting permission to set up some rather delicate scenes.

The opening sequence was to be at Manchester airport. Ray went to see the airport authorities to ask whether Jasper Carrott could use their airport and its facilities to make a comedy film.

First it was all sweetness and light. Tousle-haired Jolly Ray assured them that the airport would certainly be shown favourably, that no harm would come to anyone and that we'd show the utmost respect to the authorities. The sanctity of airports would be respected at all costs.

The next moment he was asking if it would be all right to have a plane on the tarmac, five sheepdogs rounding up several hundred panicking passengers, a blind pilot tapping his way across the runway with a white stick, and an old woman going berserk and being dragged forcibly up the plane steps, gagged, blindfolded and bound up in a horse harness.

Somehow this didn't give much credibility to our claim that the airport wouldn't be seen in a dubious light.

But Jolly Ray – he has such a *sweet* face – qualmed their fears by saying he knew it *sounded* bad but really it was just a series of *super* wheezes. I suppose that's why he's a producer.

The first day of filming saw a lot of worried airport officials buying vast quantities of Valium and main-lining Park Drive.

To start with, a beat-up Austin Cambridge arrived at the airport, screeched to a halt with great difficulty and out piled three yobboes, played by Terry, Bernard and myself. Then they careered through the airport, clinging to a trolley which was packed to the gills with cases – and with Terry, because he was sitting on top of the cases spraying beer all over the place and behaving in a revoltingly drunk manner.

This sequence took the whole day and it was complete pandemonium from beginning to end. Since I had been on holiday just before we had started shooting the film, I had to be covered in pasty white make-up to make it look as if I were an average Brummie setting off on my holiday.

So there was this pasty-faced comic lurching his way through Manchester airport, pushing a trolley at about forty miles an hour. And there was Terry, sprawled all over the cases, acting totally drunk, singing for all he was worth. Behind us was Bernard, who's about six-foot three, in a Union Jack pork pie hat and carrying a stuffed donkey – everyone brings a stuffed donkey back from Spain but Bernard's character had a friend in Spain who wanted him to take him one. . . .

Real holidaymakers were barged aside, sprayed with beer, all the while being cajoled into looking normal. Custom officials, checking-in clerks, duty officers, taken aback by this mayhem and about to protest most vigorously, would, when they heard it was for a film, stand meekly aside. I think they'd have committed hari-kari if the camera required it!

We had similar difficulties shooting our arrival in Spain. This time Jolly Ray used the favourite ploy of English producers abroad – yes, it's a travel programme, wonderful publicity for the Spanish tourist trade, get bull-fighting accepted by the RSPCA etc. Yes, Cliff Michelmore was in it, and Prince Charles.

The guy who looked after the tourist side for the Spanish authorities was English and a worrier. He was a chain smoker anyway but, from the moment that we told him about the film, he started to double chain smoke – he often had several cigarettes alight at the same time.

When he was actually watching us shoot, he just ran out of orifices for his cigarettes. He realized that something awful was about to happen but he couldn't quite understand what.

We had decided that, for the arrival in Spain, my character Sago would be legless, having drunk solidly on the plane. Sago would have to be carried down the steps by Terry, who was already pretty far gone when they had all left England. They were to be followed by Bernard, who only drank Vimto.

So the first thing the Spaniards saw was two drunks staggering down the steps of the plane, being piled on to a trolley and wheeled through the customs – upside down. We were all being extremely noisy and belligerent. Bernard was still clutching his stuffed donkey.

Everyone kept saying to the Spaniards, who were now looking rather perturbed, 'It's English humour, it's like Monty Python! Michelmore's on soon. Prince Charles has been slightly held up at the Palace.'

Take three: Mel über Alles

The holiday camp where we shot much of 'Carrott del Sol' was most bizarre. It was just as if an English holiday camp had been lifted up and transferred to the Costa del Sol. Although there were other nationalities there, like Germans, Dutch, and Belgians and French, there was something peculiarly English about the place – almost as if all the people there had agreed that 'when in Spain, do as the English do'.

The guy who ran that camp was a remarkable bloke and very funny. His name was Mel.

Mel could speak five languages and he had to because, although the camp was basically English, there were a lot of foreigners and obviously most of them didn't speak English.

So Mel would get up on stage and do bingo in five different languages. He only needed two jokes an evening because, by the time he'd told them five times over, he'd done his two hours. As he told the same joke yet again, little pockets of individual nationalities would laugh as he reached the punchline.

Mel used to run an 'It's a Knockout' competition at the camp and although the prizes weren't much –

a squeaky duck, or a night out for two in the buffet restaurant – it was really important to win. It was a big nationalistic thing – everyone went for broke.

And most enthusiastic of all were – surprise, surprise – the Germans. They'd pick their best, most athletic team and then they'd train, discuss tactics and go in with an absolute will to win. They particularly wanted to give the British a good hiding in the process.

Mel used to get into trouble with them – they always thought that he was favouring the British. Well, it was true that he did give them a *little* help now and then because, while everyone else was trying like hell, the British were in for the hell of it. They'd have some sixteen stone bloke in the wheelbarrow race – and he'd be the barrow!

There was one famous occasion that Mel tells about when, by some wild freak of chance, the Germans came second to the British. One of the German men accused Mel of cheating – he came up with some pathetic claim that it was unfair that, in the three-legged race, he and his partner should have had their outside legs tied together rather than their inside ones.

Mel denied this at the time but the German wouldn't let it drop. Later that evening, he was in the bar having a drink when the man came up and tried to continue the argument.

Now by this time, Mel had had enough. He had a couple of drinks inside him and he gave as good as he got. They had a blazing row in the middle of the floor which ended with the German storming off to bed with Mel screaming 'Drop dead!' after him.

Not a wise thing to say, it later turned out. The next morning, one of the girls working at the camp came running up to Mel deathly white – they'd found this German in his chalet, dead. Lying in his bed, brown bread. Mel rushes down to see what's happened and there, sure enough, is the man he had the row with dead on his bed, having had a heart attack or something overnight.

So Mel rings up the Spanish authorities and says, 'Look we've got this dead German here. Can you send someone along?' And they say yes but it would take a bit of time – because apparently this happens quite a lot, which puzzled Mel a bit.

The trouble was that it was very hot and the body began to pen a bit – and anyway they needed the room. So Mel pops down to the kitchen and clears a bit of space in the deep freeze. Then he gets a couple of blokes, sworn to secrecy, and they all go back to the chalet with a stretcher. A few minutes later there's this procession through the camp – they had covered the German with a couple of blankets and some cardboard boxes so that it looked as if they were taking some kitchen goods across.

But you can't disguise a stretcher as easily as that.

'Flogged all your trollies then, Mel?' they were yelling as he went by.

'What you got under there – a dead kraut?'

Yes, someone actually said that.

'Yes,' said Mel weakly. '*Wienerschnitzel* for dinner again.'

But they eventually got the body into the deep freeze and Mel told everyone on the camp staff who knew about it to keep mum. So they all went about their own business while waiting for the Spanish authorities to come.

During the day, people who had been in the bar the previous night were coming up to Mel and saying, 'That German was out of order last night.'

'Yeah, well,' Mel would say, 'he had a good point. You mustn't condemn him out of hand – he was just being honest. Don't speak ill of the – er – don't speak ill of the Germans.'

What Mel didn't know was that three or four of the camp staff had been ordered to make about forty pizzas for a barbeque in a couple of night's time. Two of the girls had been given the pizzas to put away. And there was only one place to keep them – the deep freeze.

So the two girls march into the kitchen with this huge pile of pizzas and when they get down to the deep freeze, one of them manages to hold her pizzas with one hand and lift up the lid with the other. She's just about to put her pizzas in when she sees this big lump under a sheet. She tries to pull it out of the way and the next thing she knows is she's staring into the face of this brown bread German. So she drops her pizzas and just about manages to tell her friend that she'd better put hers down. Which the friend does, takes a look – and immediately faints.

The girls go screaming through the camp, yelling, 'Mel, Mel, there's a dead German in the deep freeze! A dead German – there's a dead German in –'

And Mel's going, 'Sssh! Ssssh!' And saying to the campers, in all seriousness, 'It's an English phrase. An English phrase for venison.'

Take four:
Sago bolognese

Several major scenes that we planned for 'Carrott del Sol' worked well on the spot but failed on film for technical reasons. It was no one's fault in particular – in fact, we did the best that we could – but in the end, it came down to the question of feasibility.

For certain scenes to be successful, we would have needed four cameras and a number of microphones to pick up every reaction shot of the characters involved – an extremely expensive operation. Even then, we had no guarantee of success since we were relying on the public and our own ability to ad lib within a situation.

For me, one of the scenes that worked best but was never seen was one that we set up in the camp restaurant.

Mel had explained to us that there was a buffet lunch there every day and you could always tell the newcomers at the camp by the way they behaved.

The first time they had lunch there, they would get their plate and go round the trestle tables picking a little bit of pastrami and macaroni, some salad, potatoes – they were a quarter of the way round and they would discover they had a full plate. So they would go back to get another plate and would be a bit more choosy this time, going down the line again.

By the time they were halfway round the table, they had two full plates and a lot more than they actually wanted.

On the basis that it was all paid for however much you took, things like apples, oranges and bread rolls would be surreptitiously smuggled into handbags and jacket pockets to be taken back to the chalets for consumption later.

It was only after a day or two that people began to realize that it wasn't a locust job – get as much down as possible before it all goes – but that there was always food and wine left if you wanted to go back for more.

When Mel told us about this, it occurred to us that we could use it for a couple of candid camera type scenes, with hidden cameras and microphones.

First of all I wanted to exploit the comic potential in the real distrust, fear and even dislike that some British holidaymakers have for their German counterparts. It's an undeniable fact that the image of the average German on holiday as a beer-swilling, poolside chair-grabbing lout is one held by a lot of British tourists.

The fact that there are hundreds of British yobboes like Sago and the gang who are throwing up in Torremolinos and brawling in Benidorm seems to escape them.

To convey the fear and prejudice between the two sets of holidaymakers, director Terry Ryan thought it would be amusing to persuade a couple of dozen campers to wear Hitler moustaches and sit around like little Adolfs in the restaurant. This would give our three yobboes the chance to show up their ignorant prejudice.

Once again, when the idea of appearing on camera was mentioned, people fell over themselves to get into the act. So we had eighty-year-old grandmas, middle-aged dads, a few kids and even a dog sitting eating their buffet lunch with black tufts of hair glued to their upper lip.

Bernard, Terry and myself were filmed peering into the restaurant from the outside.

'But how d'you know they're Germans?' said Sago.

'I dunno,' said Terry. 'They just sort of *look* like Germans.'

Meanwhile some of the British tourists were getting carried away – dress up the average English person in disguise and they soon lose any shyness or reserve they might have. So some of them were soon goose-stepping up and down the restaurant, *Zieg Heil*-ing to mini-Nuremberg rallies and commandeering dinner trollies for the Luftwaafe.

Strangely, the German holidaymakers watching this weird behaviour found it most amusing.

'Look, Gerda,' one said to his wife. 'Ze Britishers are having eine Adolf look-alike buffet.'

But it was on the first day of the three yobboes' holiday that we set up a scene based on their complete inability to understand the ways things worked at the buffet.

The three of us staggered around the table piling food on to our plates and then dumped ourselves down at a pre-arranged table, where, not suspecting that there were two cameras and microphones trained on them, two couples – one Belgian and one German – were sitting.

On our plates was a grotesque amount of food: something like two large pieces of chicken on each, covered in spaghetti bolognese, with prawns, tomatoes, paella and green salad.

Terry tottered along behind with three litre bottles of wine, an empty glass and one hard-boiled egg – that was his lunch.

Not surprisingly, the two couples were a little taken aback by this sight.

We introduced ourselves in a typical way – '*Vive le Deutschland*', 'Did I see you at Wembley in '66?' and all that – and then for the next half hour, we set out to be as ignorant and gross as is humanly possible.

As we started to eat these enormous platefuls, the two men at the table, who must have been disturbed by what was going on, didn't bat an eyelid – and they talk about the English having reserve! On the other hand, the German woman did express some surprise at the amounts we had.

'All is for you?'

'Aye, the lot,' I said. 'You've got to get it down you before all the foreigners get here. Once them foreigners get here, they'll nick everything. They won't leave anything except the rice – I don't think they like rice, foreigners.'

Then I noticed that the German woman hadn't finished her chicken and had left some spaghetti bolognese on the side. When she put her knife and fork down, I looked at her and then at her plate.

'Have you finished?'

'*Ja, dank*. Very nice.'

'And you're leaving all that?'

'*Ja*, very nice but I've had enough.'

I looked at her plate again, with its remnants on the side.

'Could I have your plate?'

'You want that?'

'Yes, yes,' I said hungrily and, reaching over for her plate, I scraped what was left of her spaghetti bolognese off her plate on to mine. Then I took her chicken and scraped the rest of the meat off it.

While all this was going on, her husband was still eating and he happened to put his fork down for a moment. Whereupon Bernie leant across and took his plate, which still had a good half chicken on it and some spaghetti bolognese, and scraped it all on to his own plate. The German bloke, who clearly hadn't finished, didn't say a word.

Then a waitress came over – this was completely unplanned – and asked us whether we'd like any drinks, and Bernie said he'd like an orange juice.

'Uno orang-o,' I said to the waitress. 'Yes-o, you-o go-o to get-o my mate-o an orange-o.'

'Have you got any brasso?' added Terry who was now completely legless having been bottling into his wine. (Of course, the wine was real and Terry, who had been keyed up about the whole scene, just drank it without thinking.)

After a couple of minutes, the waitress returned with the drink, put it down on the table and said, 'Thirty *pesetas*, please.' We all looked at each other and realized at the same time that none of us had any money because we'd all got stage clothes on. And just then we all clocked what we could do with this. We turned to the two couples.

'Excuse me,' I said. 'We have no money for the orange-o.' They looked a bit puzzled, so I said, 'No *pesetas*. For the orange-o. Have you any *pesetas*?'

For a moment, there was complete disbelief on their faces. Then, without a word, the German woman reached for her purse and the German bloke stood up to get some money out of his trouser pocket. They both held out some money – there was a hundred *peseta* note and a fifty *peseta* piece and the Belgians gave me some as well – so I took the money off them, paid the waitress the thirty pesetas and put the rest of the money in my pocket. They all looked totally bemused, but they still never said a word – and never asked for the money back.

When the German couple finally got up to go, we made a point of standing up to say good-bye – we told them that we'd forgotten the war and that we were all friends now which seemed to please them. Then, as they were going, I sneaked three bread rolls off the table and wrapped them up in a serviette.

'Psst,' I went as loudly as I could, holding the flap of my jacket out to hide them from the waitress. They just stood looking aghast, as I went 'Psst, psst! Take these for later!'

Now everyone was looking and the German couple were backing towards the door going, 'No. No. No, *dank*. No.'

And I was saying, 'Bread rolls. For later. Psst! Have the bread rolls – it's all right. They no-o see-o. For your chalet-o.'

But the couple just kept going and, as they were leaving the restaurant still saying, 'No. No. No,' I furtively looked round and then shoved the rolls up my jumper. At this, the Belgian woman, who was still at the table, finally burst out into hysterical laughter – she'd found us pretty funny throughout lunch, and now she just sat there and heaved.

I'd been struggling to stop myself laughing for the last half hour and at this, I just cracked up as well. In the end the four of us were sitting there howling with laughter and everyone else in the restaurant was turning round to see what was happening.

The only person who had a completely straight face was the Belgian husband who didn't have a clue what was going on. He was still trying to work out how an orange-o had cost 500 *pesetas*.

After it was all over, someone went to find the German couple, explained what had been going on and bought them a bottle of champagne. They were very good about it and gave us permission to use the film. They were asked if they'd had any suspicions as to what was going on. No, they said, they had been to the camp before and were quite used to the English!

As for the Belgian couple, there really was not much we could do after we'd all collapsed laughing. So once we'd pulled ourselves together a bit, we took the Belgian woman aside and pointed in the direction of one of the hidden cameras – one of the crew took the cover away and there it was. Then we told her to turn round and there was a camera behind her as well.

She couldn't stand it – she just burst out laughing again.

Take five: The big celebrity goat

Why we needed a goat was never too clear, but it seemed to be completely logical at the time.

We were planning to shoot a scene at Puerto Banus, which is a very trendy part of Marbella and definitely the place to be seen at – the in-place on Marbella, in fact. In the film, Sago and the others were trying to raise some money, and decided to go to Puerto Banus, find an animal and take photographs of tourists with it.

Now this was a rather unsavoury trade in the town. Local people would have some unfortunate chimpanzee or lion cub, and they'd charge tourists a fortune to have their photographs taken with it. It was pretty nasty since they used to drug their animals and, once the lion cubs became too big to handle, they would apparently just kill them off.

So our three characters decided to use a goat, which meant we had to go and hire one off somebody. This was easier said than done since goats are highly valued by the rural community – there is a lot of money in goats.

Eventually Roger the go-for – if you wanted anything bizarre, you'd get Roger and somehow he would find it for you – had to go to a village in the mountains where he persuaded someone to hire us his goat.

Apparently this bloke was very suspicious but finally relented, after Roger had sworn allegiance to the Catholic Church, St Francis of Assisi, and King Carlos, and let him go off with his goat, accompanied by his son who was aged about ten or eleven.

For some obscure reason – but, again, it made perfect sense at the time – we were dressed up as Arabs. So for two days, the three of us, badly disguised in Arab gear, were leaping about Puerto Banus with this goat, to get people to agree to be photographed with it – and pay good money for the privilege.

We had one or two problems here. And, since the Spaniards are not particularly overawed by the camera, there were times when they took exception to the disruption being caused.

What we had not foreseen was that, because the goat was from a rural area, it was not particularly used to traffic – in fact, something like a moped scared it out of its wits. Every time a 50cc Honda went by, the goat would leap in the air, crapping and pissing itself empty all over the trendy boutiques, bars and restaurants of the town.

A further problem was that, since this was a nanny goat, there came a moment later in the day when it needed milking – and the farmer's son, who was chaperoning it, had taken the opportunity of his day out to throw himself in the harbour and narrowly escape drowning.

So someone had to milk the goat. There was, of course, only one person for the job – Roger. We had long discussions about how exactly you milk a goat – right tit, left tit, both tits at once – and, at last, Roger went to work with a large enamel bucket.

After a lot of coaxing, the goat delivered about enough milk to cover a Weetabix. We all gave an ironic cheer and Roger returned to his milking position – head stuck under the animal's belly – and started whispering sweet nothings and words of encouragement.

Fate's timing is rarely amiss. At precisely that moment, a Harley Davidson 1000cc Black Panther hammered up at one million revs, passing within feet of where we were standing.

The goat reacted like an effluence discharge pipe all over Roger – and, of course, the camera wasn't running!

In the meantime, word had got round the goat's village as to why it had been hauled away in an expensive Range-Rover by an English follower of St Francis of Assisi. The goat was going to be a star.

So when Roger, covered in every excretion known to goat, returned to the village after the first day's filming, all hell broke loose: the road was lined with local people clapping and cheering. Some of them were just trying to touch the goat.

The next morning when he came by to collect it, they were out on the streets again, wishing the goat well by kissing it on the head. That day, Roger was allowed to take it on his own in the Range-Rover – the big celebrity goat.

Take six: Que?

In the middle of a square in Marbella are a number of tables that are served by five or six restaurants – and, on one occasion by a particularly smarmy Spanish waiter called Miguel.

Miguel was an almost foolproof disguise that I used on a couple of occasions during the shooting of 'Carrott del Sol'. I could walk around the camp and no one would know who I was. I'd walk straight past my wife or the entire film crew and no one would recognize me.

I wore a wig and a moustache, and dressed in a bright red shirt, black slim trousers, a medallion and a heavy wrist watch that I'd borrowed. I'd do a lot of heel-stamping and finger-clicking and, whenever possible, I'd explain that I'd fallen through an *olé* in the floor (very bad Spanish joke).

I suppose I looked like the Englishman's idea of a typical greasy dago because the only people who looked twice were Spaniards. They reacted as if I were a nutter on the bus, a Spanish nutter on the bus. Anybody who looked that Spanish had *got* to be a nutter.

When we set up a table in the middle of the square, we were hoping and praying that some English people would sit down at it so that Miguel could serve them in front of the hidden cameras.

Our prayers were answered. A young English couple came along with their two children. I came out and they ordered something like a beer, a tomato juice and two Cokes.

I went into a very bad Spanish act, pointing at my watch. '*Espredanti dindare y ventipes salantare cara macari a una hore mangere,*' I was saying. It was lunchtime and I was most emphatic that they should eat.

'No,' the husband said in a typical no-nonsense British way. 'No, we are not hungry. We would just like a beer, a tomato juice and two Coca-Colas.'

'*Ele cervente uno uno. Manger, manger? Parlez français?*'

'We would like a beer, a tomato juice and two coca-colas.'

'Okay, okay,' I said. '*Benissimo sedentrimo bene due Cocas.*' And looking at their little boy, '*Bene, bene eesa Bobbee Charlton, bene!*'

So I walked off with their order and came back a minute later with a candle and lit it – in the full midday sun. Then I came back with the drinks, talking all the time.

'*Ente imorente eh una hore mange benissimo paella ono carrucina vida.*'

And they were getting worried.

'What's he saying?'

'I don't know what he's saying. Don't ask me.'

'Just keep saying "no", that's all.'

'*Eh cora idayo Bobbee Charlton fantastico. Bene Eusebio!*'

Then I started laying the table, banging knives and forks down in front of them.

'No,' they were going, panic setting in. 'No eat. Just drink.'

'Icidente una hore benissimo mangare eesa Bobbee Charlton fantastico.'

'I knew we shouldn't have come here. I mean, it's lunchtime and you're supposed to eat here.'

'Well, we're not going to. No. No *eat!*'

Finally I came out with a great steaming plate of paella, together with huge salads.

'No,' they're saying, 'we're *not* going to pay for it. We have not ordered it. We are not going to pay for it.'

'Oh, they don't understand at all.'

Then they began discussing the situation under their breath.

'You write to your mother,' he was saying, 'and tell her we're going to be a bit delayed and I'll hide the camera and the baked beans.'

'Yes,' said his wife. 'I'll smuggle a file into the kids' stuffed donkey and I'll try and sew a picture of the Queen into my plimsolls.'

'Buon appetito,' I'm saying, *'sullte mente cinque cente mille pesetas. Bene, bene. Eesa GRANDE Bobbee Charlton.'*

Finally the man twigged that something was going on. He asked me, in all seriousness, if I'd ever heard of 'Fawlty Towers'.

'Que?' I answered, quick as a flash. Too quickly, it gave us away. . . .

Take seven: Talent Night

We decided to stage a talent contest for 'Carrott del Sol'. The camp used to have the occasional talent night but, unbeknown to anyone except the organizers, this was going to be rather different because Terry, Bernard and myself were all going to perform.

We planned some pretty classy entertainment. Terry was going to do terrible impressions of Eddie Waring and James Cagney, Bernard would do his party piece, which was actually diving into a glass of water. Then I would come on as Sago and do his bad, crass Brummie stand-up comic act. I was also going to appear as the Spanish waiter from down the road who would come on and play ethnic flamenco music on his guitar.

So on the night we had a whole international audience there expecting a genuine talent contest – and I must admit it was all pretty rough. Before we came on there were some awful sights – some really abysmal acts. We thought we were bad but we were totally overshadowed by the first act, which was five Dutchmen doing the can-can. The Dutch appear to have a penchant for displaying bare arses – why, I don't know. Perhaps it's from all that bending down, sticking their fingers in dykes. Five sunburnt Dutch arses are not a pretty sight. In fact, it was about as subtle as a bull mastiff in a poodle parlour.

Then there was a very bad singer from Eastbourne who regularly changed key before the resident band, which was backing him, had worked out what he was singing. I think he was trying either for 'My Way' or possibly 'San Francisco' but the words and the melody got mixed up so that he ended up with something like 'I Did It in San Francisco'.

And everyone was watching this appalling show, clapping and cheering for all they were worth. Holidaymakers are prepared to accept almost anything if it's done with effort.

I came on first as Miguel, having been introduced by Mel as a typical flamenco guitarist and singer. I bowled out, completely unrecognizable in my disguise and proceeded to give them about five or six minutes of appalling noise, playing the one flamenco riff I learnt years ago over and over again, and singing in terrible strangulated cod Spanish.

There was obviously a smattering of Spaniards in the audience because they were laughing at all this stamping of feet, slapping of the guitar and this godawful wailing. However, everybody else listened very politely in the obvious belief that they were listening to genuine Spanish flamenco folk singing and when I had finished, they applauded and whistled and yelled for more. The can-canning Dutchmen must have softened them up, I suppose.

Then it was Terry's turn and, to an audience that was four-fifths non-British, he started doing his impressions of Eddie Waring and James Cagney. This didn't get much of a reaction so he tried Eddie Waring doing James Cagney. Then he went into a John Wayne routine: 'Okay, get off your milk and drink your horse,' and so on. He finished with a highly forgettable solo performance on the penny whistle.

Not even the English laughed this time and the rest of the audience didn't know what the hell was going on. As he left the stage to waves of healthy apathy, Mel came bounding on full of holiday-camp bonhomie.

'Wasn't he *fabulous*?' he said.

Later Bernard dived into his glass and nearly broke his neck doing it – that got quite a laugh. And finally I came on as Sago.

Even by Sago's standards, I was truly awful – although some people say it was the finest perform-ance I've ever given.

I went into this really terrible routine, starting it with, 'Good evening, ladies and gentlemen and those that have had the operation. On my way here tonight. . . .'

Then just to finish off any foreigner there who thought he understood basic English, I told them the joke about the man who goes for a job on a building site, whose foreman has a bit of a stutter, and was called Donkey.

'H-h-have y-y-y-you g-g-got a b-b-billy c-c-can?' asks the foreman.

'No, not yet.'

'W-w-well, I c-c-can g-g-get y-y-you a b-b-billy c-c-can. H-h-have y-y-you g-g-got a d-d-donkey j-j-jacket?'

'No, I've never been in the building trade.'

'I c-c-can g-g-get y-y-you a d-d-donkey j-j-jacket. Where's y-y-your sh-sh-shovel?'

'I haven't got that either.'

'W-w-well, I'll g-g-get y-y-you one when I g-g-get the d-d-donkey j-j-jacket and the b-b-billy c-c-can.'

'Oh thanks very much, Donkey.'

'Who t-t-told y-y-you t-t-to c-c-call m-m-me D-D-Donkey?'

'The bloke over there on the JCB.'

'Well, hee haw hee haw hee haw t-t-to m-m-mind his own b-b-b-business.'

After my performance, I was collared by a Belgian professor of English who wanted that particular joke explained.

'What noise does a donkey make?' I asked.

'Yaw! Yaw!' said the Belgian.

I didn't try to explain further.

However 'Carrott del Sol' finally worked out – some people found it funny but the majority didn't – I still strongly believe in that approach to humour. I'm convinced that there is a great field of comedy to be explored in what you might call 'situation ad lib' – if only one could sort out the enormous cost problems involved.

Because we're all becoming aware of what scripted comedy is about, it's very difficult to surprise people any more – and surprise is one of the basic elements of comedy.

In personal career terms, there's no doubt it was quite a risk for me. Normally the scripted material I use on television has, I know, a fair chance of working because I have used it before in the theatre. But when you go out to ad lib, just hoping and praying that things will turn up that will enable you to stimulate comedy out of a situation that is completely unrehearsed and unscripted, then you run the risk of falling flat on your face.

Even so, I was glad to have had the chance to live for a while on Carrott del Sol.

7 Wild and Dangerous

The Big Yin and tonic

Billy Connolly and myself are often compared, although both of us are adamant that we don't approach comedy in the same way. But I can see that because we both come from the same grass-root folk club background, there are similarities in our styles.

It was an incident in an Edinburgh bar that once brought home to me the great differences that lie between Billy's and my approach.

I was up in Edinburgh at the time of the festival for a seminar which was part of a general meeting of the people running British television. They have this three-day conference, the mornings of which are spent in serious discussion about really important media issues: is television a good thing? Does 'Coronation Street' genuinely offer art to the masses? Can anything be done about the flavour of the crisps in the Television Centre canteen?

By about mid-day, everybody is nicely dropping off because they haven't got to bed until at least four o'clock in the morning. I always think that they ought to hold TV conferences at three a.m. in the hotel bar – they'd get a much better attendance.

I had been invited to speak at a seminar on light entertainment along with Bob Monkhouse, John

Lloyd and Dudley Moore. It was strange to see how, after his great success in Hollywood, Dudley Moore was held in great awe by everyone – we were all hanging on his every word. He'd be wondering out loud where to put his coat and everyone would solemnly write down what he had said and how he said it.

I find that when television people get together, there is a lot of in-talking and gossip. You also begin to realize the amazing number of drunks in the business – very famous drunks. People on television are, in fact, just very famous drunks. They are permanently ratted. I think that's why they are so confident – when you're that ratted, you know no fear.

I soon fell into these ways quite comfortably.

So it was in this hotel bar one lunch-time that I remember having a chat with Billy. Although he was not participating in the seminar, he was up in Edinburgh for the festival and had joined up with quite a large group of television people in the bar.

The place was packed. The seminars had just finished for the morning and, since they all worked in television, all these ratted people had raced round to the nearest bar as soon as they got out.

We'd been there for a while, jammed solid in this bar, when I offered to buy a round of drinks. Although I do struggle hard to keep up the tradition-al, mean comic image, I'd bought one in January and it was now September so I thought it was my turn again.

So I started to try to find my way through this mass of people to the bar to buy a round for about six people, including Billy.

In the distance, I could see the four barmen

working away behind the bar. The head one was wearing standard hotel barman gear – he was bursting out of his shirt and his bow-tie was all askew.

It appears to be a rule in hotels that they issue uniforms two sizes too small for overweight staff and three sizes too big for the skinny, anorexic ones. Hence the fat barmen are purple and bursting while the thin barmen seem, well, a bit draughty.

Since it was a very hot September, these barmen were spraying everyone with perspiration, running up and down behind the bar like bright red lawn sprinklers. As they went by, people were yelling out things like, 'Four Cinzanos with a twist of lemon and a Buck's Fizz,' because it's very important at these gatherings not to order anything ordinary. So they'll ask for one Jamaican Road Drill, a Tasmanian Lobe Squeezer and a Hawaiian Papa Doc Juice. They only ask for a gin and tonic if they can have something exotic in it like a paw-paw or a sculpted yam.

These Scottish barmen, who were used to 'Four pints o' heavy and a triple scotch', were getting a bit uptight as they had to work out these ridiculous orders and find straws, frills, and bits of exotic tropical fruit. By the time I had worked my way to the bar, which took about ten minutes, they were more than a little brassed off.

They were sweating away and pounding up and down the bar, banging down glasses everywhere, and the angrier the people waiting became, the more the barmen banged and stomped and sweated and pounded.

Meanwhile I'm going 'Ahem, Ahem', as they went by me with the speed of the ball at the Wimbledon final and it was obviously useless – they were never going to answer to a polite cough. So, summoning up a bit more bottle, I say, 'Two pints of bitter and one –' but no luck.

Five minutes later, and I'm still there waiting and by now people are getting served all around and over my head so I'm beginning to lose my temper a bit.

I don't know why I'm losing control because, in fact, this is quite a usual occurrence for me. I have the greatest difficulty in ever getting served at a bar.

It was once explained to me that there is a manual for barmen which contains a description and identi-kit picture of a potentially difficult customer and instructions as to how to detect and ignore him. Yes – I look like that person.

I had been trying the same order in a Scottish accent and holding two £5 notes in my hands but that didn't seem to be working either.

'Tae pints o' bitter and a wee scotch a' lemon,' I'd be saying, but it was still Borg to McEnroe, back-hand return from McEnroe as they pounded up and down the bar in front of me.

So then I get more money out and I'm holding a bunch of £5 notes in each hand, shouting, 'Will *anybody* serve me tae pints o' bitter and a wee –' By the time I had got my American Express card, Barclaycard, Access Card in one hand and £50 in the other, I'm beginning to get really annoyed and still the barmen are ignoring me as they rush up and down the bar.

Just then, I heard Billy's voice from about ten foot back from the bar. It's a voice that barmen notice.

'Hey, pal,' he was yelling. 'Hae ye got any change for the cigarette machine?'

All the barmen immediately stopped what they were doing and there was a mad scramble to the tills to see who could get the change first. McEnroe won.

Meanwhile I'm staring with disbelief at the disruption. I must have looked pathetic, clutching a handful of fivers and cards and with a mouthful of glacé cherries – well, you have to do something while you're waiting.

McEnroe stared at me. Now was my chance. Quickly I gabble my order, 'Two pints of bitter, a scotch, a dry martini and tonic, two glasses of red wine and a large Ruritanian mango.'

'Can you pass this change to the big fella at the back, Jimmy?'

And not wanting to lose the effect of the cards and fivers, I say, 'Why, yes . . . yes, of course. Put it in my mouth and I'll transfer it back gladly.'

Somehow that sums up the difference between Billy and myself.

Anarchy evening

I never knew there was such a thing as an 'anarchy evening' until I recently heard my old friend Ian Hone describing one in gruesome detail.

Ian is the manager and driving force behind a club in Birmingham called The Opposite Lock. A while ago, they decided to open up an extension next door which they called King Arthur's Court. There, for a set sum, you can get a medieval feast – about ninety courses, mead, wenches, strolling olde worlde minstrels from Solihull, that sort of thing.

One evening Ian invited me to observe the proceedings at King Arthur's Court since he knew I was looking for new material.

It was certainly an evening of alternative entertainment.

The strolling minstrels that evening could only be described as a Buck's Fizz clone. The oldest song they sang was 'Jumping Jack Flash' – and they played it on a lute.

But the key to the whole evening is the mead. It's a warm, sweet-tasting wine which everyone knocks back as if it were Ribena and, after about an hour, they're reeling all over the place. Very powerful stuff, mead.

The frivolity always starts with bread roll missiles. Ingenious medieval stone-throwing devices, constructed from hairbands and bent spoons, propel lumps of Mother's Pride at great velocity towards some unsuspecting foe. There are cries of 'Yea verily, varlet!' and 'Avaunt, ye blackguards!' and 'Hey, you bastard – that hurt!'

Halfway through the masses of courses, the chicken legs start going over the shoulder à la Henry VIII. After that, anything goes.

They have some medieval stocks there as well. There's no particular plan as to who is going to end up in the stocks, but somehow you can always pick the guy who will. He's paid his ticket and he's there like everyone else but, there's no two ways about it, when you're one of life's losers, there's just no escaping it. You're a loser and that's that.

You can pick him out at the beginning of the evening. He'll normally have glasses, dandruff and carefully parted brilliantined hair, with three or four strands sticking up at the back. When you spot him, you do so with a relieved sigh because you know he's the one that'll be in the stocks, not you.

By this time, everyone in the room also knows who the loser is so the relief is catching. It helps the evening along.

When they get round to popping him in the stocks, it's all mild, good-humoured fun. They fling bits of bread and remains of chicken and everyone laughs – including the loser because he doesn't know what's coming next. Into the face goes the old Black Forest gâteau, smear it down his chest and – whoops! – who poured the mead down his trousers?

By now, the loser is beginning to look as if he has just come from a 'Tiswas' audition.

But mead plays strange tricks on the imagination. Several people really start to believe that the loser was the man who killed their king, Richard the Lionheart – their beloved sovereign, slain by this savage! They sometimes have to be disarmed and physically restrained from pouring boiling Nescafé into his eye sockets.

However, this kind of frivolity is distinctly seasonal. Hot mead, hot ale, hot chicken and hot rolls tend not to be so popular in the summer months. So Ian now shuts down the place for a while until the next medieval season.

Last year he started to hire out King Arthur's Court during the quiet months to anyone who could make use of the premises for an evening's entertainment. For a time, he advertised in the local papers and it all worked quite well. He had them all there – trad bands, gay romantics, the Psychedelic Glee Club.

Then, one day, he had this call from a group. They were called The Gobboes, and they wanted to use the club for a musical soirée. Or, as they put it, an anarchy evening.

Ian was a bit taken aback by this – he hadn't had too many anarchy evenings at the club – but times were difficult and, after all, he'd seen everything at this place from the local Billy Graham organization to the Count Basie Band. So, he thought, what the hell – let them have their anarchy evening.

He keeps a look-out for ads in the local papers – 'Come and enjoy an anarchy evening with The Gobboes,' 'The Gobboes in Concert', something like that – but there's no announcement at all. So he's more than a little surprised when a van rolls up on the afternoon of the booking and out step The Gobboes.

When he sees them, Ian begins to get a bit apprehensive. Because there was no getting round it – The Gobboes were certainly an aggressive-looking bunch.

As their name suggested, they gobbed a lot in every direction and clearly had very little respect for authority. During the course of what passed for a conversation with them, Ian came to the conclusion that they had a very definite philosophy of life – if they couldn't punch it, drink it, smoke it or screw it, they weren't interested.

A little bit worried by now, Ian goes back to his office while they set up their equipment. He comes back just as they started rehearsing and has great difficulty leaving the room because he's pinned up against the wall by the noise. He escapes with his eardrums just about intact and returns to his office which, like the rest of the street, is shaking by now in time to The Gobboes.

If this is what the group's like, Ian's thinking, God help us when their followers get here.

Just to nip any unpleasantness in the bud, he waits outside in Gas Street at a little before eight o'clock, when the gig is due to start.

By half-past eight, no one has arrived and Ian's beginning to think that what could have become another Toxteth has been avoided when he hears a distant chugging noise. Over the horizon comes an old Ford Zephyr – obviously the winner of a recent stock car survival race. Inside the car, he can count at least eight heads.

They pull up outside King Arthur's Court.

'Oy!' one of the blokes in the car yells to Ian. 'Is this where The Gobboes are playin'?'

Ian nods, gulping slightly.

The Zephyr pulls into the side and eight yobs scramble out. If Ian was nervous when he saw The Gobboes, he's now well into a major wobbly. Because these dudes are about Anarchy with a capital 'A'.

They are wearing heavy leather jackets with big steel studs, proclaiming 'ANARCHY – GOBBOES RULE', 'REVOLUTION' and 'SCREW THE PIGS'. They all have badges with 'I DON'T GIVE A FART!', 'THE KRAYS ARE INNOCENT' and 'SHOVE THE LAW UP YOUR ARSE'. And so on.

By the time these Brummie Che Guevaras are making their way towards the club door, Ian is sweating profusely. As they barge past him, they're saying things like, 'You don't let pooftahs into this dump, do you?' and 'You'd better serve Ansells Mild here – else there's trouble.'

They're all milling around the door and, by now, Ian is seriously considering calling in the SAS.

Just then the guy who's last out of the car and who's just slamming the door shouts after the rest of them.

'Hey, Kevin,' he yells. 'Kevin! You can't leave the car parked here – it's on a double yellow line.'

8 On My Way Here Tonight...

Under the influence

One of the questions I most often get asked is, 'Who makes you laugh?' It's always a tough one to answer because you always want to astound people by introducing them to a comedian that they had never heard of – who's terrific, will have them rolling about on the floor, and yet who's completely unknown.

Unfortunately, they don't appear to exist, at least as far as British comedy is concerned. I always like to build up the credo a bit by throwing in a few American names like George Carlin, Steve Martin and the late John Belushi – American comics are virtually unknown in this country, which is quite surprising since their standard of humour is extremely high.

Over here, if a guy is really funny, people will know about him, and in fact the comics who make me laugh are those that make everyone else laugh – the really individual comic talents like John Cleese, Eric Morecambe, Spike Milligan and Bob Monkhouse, etc.

I suppose I was about nineteen when I began to come out of my shell and was first influenced by comedy. At school, I'd always had a very vivid imagination although I'd never been anything like the school clown.

One of my best friends was Bev Bevan, whom I'd known since I was eleven, and we shared a very odd, private sense of humour. Like a lot of kids, we had a rapport and we were always laughing at things that no one else found remotely funny. Even to this day, we can be in tucks about something silly and sit sniggering in a corner much to the bewilderment of others.

After I had left school, I had become quite introverted, with a hang-up about religion and possibly an inflated sense of ego. I was something of a recluse and spent a lot of time at home not doing very much – working in a department store during the day and watching television most evenings.

Then I started going round to the house of a friend of mine, whose parents were very aware people. His mum, in particular, was interested in jazz – people like Benny Goodman and Stan Kenton – and also liked the good popular music of the time. For instance, she was a Stones fan when for most middle-aged people they were the anti-Christ.

She had a very open, interested mind and we used to spend a lot of time round there talking about the world over coffee, cheese and biscuits – and very occasionally, beer. We always knew that the time to clear out was when her old man came back in at about 10.30 – he'd give us a glare and we'd scuttle out into the night.

She used to play us some records by a man called Tom Lehrer, of whom I'd never heard until then. Initially I didn't have the faintest idea what it was about. There were one or two amusing things like 'Poisoning the Pigeons in the Park' but, apart from those, I really couldn't see anything funny there. Then I started actually to listen to them and, after the third or fourth time, the humour clicked for me.

I now know that this is true of all good comedy albums. You really need to hear them several times to appreciate them because you don't have two of the main essentials for comedy, the presence of the comic and his visual effect.

But, after I had heard Tom Lehrer a few times, I started to understand what the man was about. He was more than just a talented man who wrote very funny songs with an extremely sick sense of humour, he was also very ahead of his time. His humour was summed up very well by that wonderful quote from the *New York Times*: 'Mr Lehrer's music is not fettered by such inhibiting factors as good taste.' If someone wrote that about me, I'd be delighted.

I think what impressed me most was his wonderful chat between songs. Not only was he very funny, an excellent songwriter and an accomplished pianist, but he did this superb material between the songs, all apparently ad-libbed, although I realize now that it was well honed by the time the recorded performance took place.

It was about then that I began to realize that my sense of humour was always slightly different from the norm at that time. For example, I remember thinking The Smothers Brothers were hysterically funny when they came over to Britain – I just used to roar at them. Then they were going to do a series for the BBC but they only got to do two of them before the whole thing folded and they went back home – apparently only a few people over here found them at all funny.

I began to listen to records by other American

comics who used that raconteur style. Shelley Berman I thought was very funny and very original, and Bill Cosby. I heard the classic double album by Woody Allen a bit later and was terrifically impressed by it.

While I was listening to all these very distinctive and original American comics, working in that tradition that I liked so much, no one was really doing it in this country. No one, that is, except a guy called Blaster Bates who was an explosives expert. He was and is a very funny and highly original comic – a very underrated talent, in my view. I've never met him but I suspect that he's not famous simply because he doesn't want fame.

I also remember seeing Bob Monkhouse at around this time and being struck by the way he was clearly influenced by American stand-up comedy. I had just started compering at a folk club called The Boggery and this created a tremendous demand for material. So I used to go down to the local cabaret club to nick the odd joke or two to help with the continuity at the folk club.

Normally I would come back with about six or seven lines from the comics who appeared there, but when I saw Bob Monkhouse, I came back with about eight pages.

Of course, I've seen him perform many times since then and I have always been impressed by him. In my view, he is simply one of the top stand-up comics we have. You have to see him live to see him at his best but, when you do, you know you are looking at one who is very much what they call a 'comic's comic'.

As I spent more time compering at The Boggery, I suppose the idea of using raconteur comedy as part of my act was building unconsciously in my mind. I used to get laughs like everybody else by doing one-line gags.

Then one night at the club, thinking about what I was going to do, I realized that I had this piece on Butlin's – not a joke but simply three or four minutes about my experiences at the camp, with no punchline. I was genuinely very scared when I got to do this chat without a safe punchline to fall back on, but it went down quite successfully, so after that I started to be more experimental with my humour.

After a while I found that the introductions to my songs were longer than the songs themselves. I'd spend about ten minutes introducing a song that lasted two. Finally I dropped all pretence of their being introductions and just did funny pieces.

When I started at The Boggery, I was convinced that there would be hundreds of people on the circuit being as funny in their way as Lehrer, Cosby, Berman and the rest. When I found that they hardly existed, I started to do it myself. At first I was just copying – I did a couple of Tom Lehrer songs, for example – but then I began to develop my own material.

My comedy has always been influenced by work from other comics. After all I was brought up on BBC Radio programmes like 'Round the Horne', 'Much Binding in the Marsh' and 'Life with the Lyons', and for years I have watched traditional British comedy on television. I'm sure it has had considerable influence on my style.

But it's the raconteur approach that has undoubtedly affected me most. Occasionally I'll take a theme that someone else has touched on and, just for the hell of it, rework it in my own way.

I've always thought it a sad waste that so much good comedy is never heard by the general public because of the stigma attached to the idea of using someone else's material and developing it in your own direction. It seems to be okay if it's music that is copied, adapted or re-arranged, but comedy has to be performed by the creator or no one. A great pity, in my view.

Working folk clubs has left me with several scars that, strangely enough, have been the making of me, yet are now a real hindrance to progress.

Firstly the compact surroundings and generally poor sound equipment you find in a folk club mean working in a cramped and confined stage area, never daring to move away from the mike for fear of being more inaudible than usual.

Now, whereas most comics come out on to the stage holding the microphone and walk about with it during their act, commanding the entire stage, I tend not to move away from the mike in the centre of the stage at all. Of course, I am using the stage, but simply in a different way. The fact that I am not rushing around it but staying in one place means that what I am actually saying becomes more impor-

Then there's the whole business of one-liners. In this country, we are brought up on fast one-line jokes, usually with heavy innuendo involved. The danger for a comic is that he can come to rely on that quick one line to get him an easy laugh to get out of trouble. Then, quite often, they begin to destroy the flow of a story completely and can generally stunt your creativity as a comic.

Sometimes, when relating a story or an experience, I wish I didn't have to depend on one-liners, but they are undoubtedly a sort of safety barrier. If things have gone a bit flat, you can lift an audience up by throwing in a couple. I think that it can make people feel more comfortable – they recognize that here is a joke. There's no danger of it being a lecture or something they don't understand – it's just very obviously a joke.

Another scar from my folk club days is my guitar. For the life of me, I just cannot do without it. It almost acts as a psychological barrier between myself and the audience – a kind of one-upmanship. As if the fact that I can play the guitar and the majority of the audience cannot gives me and my comedy a sort of credibility. The guitar is more than a prop to me now – it's essential to my act.

Comedians tend to fall into two categories. There are those who were funny at school and realized then that making people laugh was a way of getting on and avoiding trouble. It gave them a standing in life which they liked so that they just carried on until making people laugh became as natural to them as breathing – natural comics in fact.

I would never classify myself as a natural comic – one of those people who is exactly the same on stage as off it. To me, the fact that I could get up on stage and make people laugh was a revelation.

It's a fact that I was never bullied at school – I didn't go through the experience of having to defuse a situation by being funny. Surviving was no problem for me at school because everyone used to ignore me. I was never anything really – never wonderful but never that bad that I was a joke. No one used to pick on me. The laughs came later.

I think I was what they call a late developer. In fact, I'm still waiting to start.

The cosmic joker

A favourite question of mine, and one that has many ramifications is: 'Does God have a sense of humour?'

It's unquestionable that, humans are humorous beings. One of the biggest insults you can ever pay anybody is to accuse him of lacking a sense of humour. You can say that he's a wife-beater, child abuser, homosexual, bestial, member of the SDP – and he will take it all philosophically. Accuse him of not having a sense of humour and he's liable to prove it by trying to beat your brains out. It really is a most emotive issue.

But if a sense of humour is God-given and we are made in His image, then one would naturally assume that God has a sense of humour too.

The problem here is the fact – and it has yet to be disproved to me – that the basis of all humour is one person being made to feel inferior to another. In other words, whatever we laugh at, the cause is basically the same: we are laughing because the butt of the joke is inferior to ourselves. I realize it's quite a sweeping statement but it does make for an interesting discussion.

Even if we laugh at ourselves, it is because we are amused by our own inferiority in relation to someone else's superiority. The comic impulse is the same.

Unfortunately, this is in direct confrontation with Christian teaching which claims that all humans are equal – none of us are superior or inferior to another. Therefore to laugh at anything is against Christian teaching.

So it's quite a paradox. Does God have a sense of humour – because, if he does, then he must be a non-Christian.

Think about it.

9 Own Goal

United we fall

I know it sounds a bit flash but, for a while, I was actually a director of Birmingham City.

In fact, I have to admit that I had difficulty coming to terms with it. After thirty years of terrace upbringing, it can be a problem becoming a director – it's all so polite and traditional.

'Terribly interesting game, isn't it?'

'I say, what a terrific throw-in!'

'Who does that little chap in the black play for?'

I found that the worst times were on match days when, as a director, you're always supposed to be unemotional and stiff upper-lipped. When Birmingham scored, I'd be yelling away and then I'd have to do a quick cover-up – I'd have this terrible cramp in my right leg.

Then, in the boardroom after the game, a totally cool, detached acceptance of the result was expected.

But, if Birmingham had lost, I'd be in such a foul mood that it would be with great difficulty and pain that I'd proffer my congratulations to the opposition. If I managed a half smile, it would be through gritted teeth.

On the other hand, if we'd won, I couldn't stop myself grinning like an idiot, even while I was playing it low-key.

'So sorry about that but Keith Birtschin doesn't normally get a hat-trick.'

Mind you, as soon as we got in the car to go back home, all hell would break loose.

'We showed the bastards! Did you see that chairman's face? Like a rabid dog on heat!'

Before I became a director, I'd be at a lot of City games just as a fan and, of course, that can get a bit hairy sometimes.

The nearest I came to getting into real trouble was an occasion when I went to Old Trafford. It was the first game of the season, Birmingham were playing Manchester United, and I thought I'd risk it – it's your life in your hands up there but I'd arm myself with a nuclear missile and I'd go. So a mate of mine and myself bought tickets at the Birmingham City ground and, on this beautiful August day, we bowled up to the Old Trafford.

The ground was absolutely jammed solid with people – 60,000 in the stands and another 2000 outside. It was just a heaving mass, a sea of red and white everywhere you looked – not a blue and white scarf in sight.

Well, there was one – it had a Birmingham City fan dangling from the end.

After about twenty minutes of the game, a minor miracle occurs. Birmingham score – away from home. This takes everyone by surprise, including Birmingham who were just getting ready to kick off again. But all the City fans – about 135 of us – who were sitting in one block of seats forgot for a moment where they were and started cheering.

For an instant, 60,000 people stared at us. Then we started to get a bit of a reaction – like 'You're going to get your —kin' heads kicked in' and so on. So all the Birmingham fans decided that they'd better cheer United and stay alive.

Unfortunately my friend was something of a rookie football fan. He used to watch rally-driving but had just changed to football because he liked the colours better or something. He was totally naive about the situation and, after everyone else had gone a bit quiet, he kept on bawling and shouting for all he was worth.

'Go on, City! Shove it in the net! Show 'em how to play the game!'

I grabbed him and was hammering him in the face in as obvious a way as I could manage.

'Look, look!' I shouted to the crowd of hostile observers, 'I'm punching his face!'

'What are you doing?' he was saying.

'I'm saving your life!'

'Eh?'

'You don't come to Old Trafford and cheer the opposition.'

'Why not?'

'Well, they just don't like it very much.'

And he tries to push me away.

'And what are *they* going to do about it?'

'They'll give you a *very* nasty talking to,' I said in disbelief.

So I tried to explain the situation to him. Fortunately, a few minutes later United equalized and I could start breathing again. A couple of minutes before halftime, they got another and I was thinking 'Terrific – I can go down to the bog now.' You daren't go down there if United are losing.

My mate follows me down. He's off to get his Bovril – the old Birmingham tradition, a Bovril at half time.

I wandered off to the bog. It takes a bit of time on match days on any ground and you've always got to be careful that no one pisses in your pocket.

When I came back, I saw him at the other end of a long cafeteria. Unfortunately he also saw me.

'Hey, Carrott!' he yells in his broadest Brummie accent. 'Carrott! They've got no cowin' Bovril!'

I was at his throat in about 0.13 of a second, hissing in his ear, 'You're from Birmingham. They'll kill you.'

'But how do they *know* I come from Birmingham?'

I smiled politely at the suspicious looks and took him back to his seat, where I once again tried to explain the way things went at Old Trafford.

I thought I'd got through to him.

'All right,' he said. 'I'll keep quiet. But you're nothing but a big girl's blouse.'

Halfway through the second half, Birmingham score again. You can never trust them to do what you want and this time they equalized. Every City fan in the stadium raised up one inch out of their seats and mumbled an almost silent 'Yahoo!'

Except dummy-face.

'That's the way to do it!' he was yelling. 'Shove it up 'em!'

Of course, by this time the Neanderthal men had caught on. They've clocked us, I was thinking, how are we going to get out of this one?

A few minutes later, it was the end of the game and Birmingham had won – 2-2. So I grabbed my friend and started trying to get him out of there.

At the big exit near where we were sitting, there

were neanderthal men looking out for Birmingham City fans.

One or two of them had been distracted for a moment – they'd found a match and had managed to light it.

But we were just coming up to them and I'm going 'Ssh! Ssh!' when he starts talking to a woman who is all dressed up in red and white.

'Hey,' he says to her. 'I thought you were lucky to get a draw there. I thought Birmingham should have had at least four or five in the second half.'

'Uuuurgh!'

A split second later and this big bloke has grabbed him by the collar and is just lifting him off the ground. Well, I thought, you've got to stick by your mate, haven't you? I was just trying to squeeze past when I realized he was so naive he was going to get away with it.

'How yer going, mate?' he was saying to the neanderthal. 'All right?'

'Urgh?'

At this moment, I grabbed him and kicked him down the stairs. His collar came away from his shirt – which highly amused the neanderthal man who tried to set light to it.

We were just walking away from the ground and I was thinking, have we done it? Suddenly I realized we still weren't wearing red and white.

But I did have a white shirt on. I pinched the ketchup from a hot dog stand and squirted it all over us.

We just about made it back to the car.

I was Trevor's double

One of my best friends in football is Trevor Francis and, strangely enough, we are quite often mistaken for one another. Terrific looking bloke, Trevor Francis!

The occasion that I remember best occurred when my manager, my tour manager and myself were driving back one very foggy night after a concert in Bristol.

We had stopped at a crossroads near Birmingham to work out just where to go next. At that moment a young bloke lurched in front of the car – he'd had a couple of drinks – went round to the side of the car where my manager was sitting and asked him if we knew the way to Stratford Road, where he lived. We did and, since it was such a nasty night, we agreed to give him a lift home.

He got in the back of the car and I drove on. He sat in silence for a while as we chatted. Then suddenly he said to me, 'Are you who I think you are?'

'Well,' I said, 'who do you think I am?'

'It is, isn't it? It's you.'

I thought there was no point in pretending.

'Yes it is,' I said. 'It's me.'

'I see you every Saturday. Every time Birming-

123

ham are at home. I'm there watching you.'

Now I'm beginning to think that this is a bit strange. I've heard of fan loyalty but to come and watch me watching a game of football seemed to be going a bit far.

'You're the fastest thing I've seen on two legs.'

Then I knew there was some mistake.

' . . . it is, isn't it? It's Trevor Francis?'

'Well, no,' I said. 'We're often mistaken for one another – particularly when we play football!'

So we all had a laugh about this.

'Yes,' he said, 'I see you every Saturday. I'm there. You're magic.'

'No, it's not me although I do agree he's a great player.'

There was silence from the back for a bit as I concentrated on driving through the fog. My manager and I started chatting about how the show had gone that evening, future concerts and so on.

The guy in the back was muttering delightedly. 'They'll never believe this at work. My friends will never believe who gave me a lift.'

At last, we got to his road and, as he got out, he asked me for a photograph. 'Could you sign it for me so that I can show it to my friends?' he said.

So I got out a photograph and signed it while all the time he's going, 'I just can't believe this. . . . My friends will never believe me.'

When I gave him the photograph, he looked decidedly disappointed.

'Oh, it's you,' he said. 'Wait till I tell my friends in the morning that you gave me a lift. Now that they will believe.'

Wha' sa' teem?

I'm pretty good at avoiding football violence – I'm usually sitting between the seats on the floor – but I did have a very narrow escape in Glasgow one time.

I was doing a programme for Radio Clyde and the day I was up there just happened to be the local derby between Glasgow Celtic and Glasgow Rangers.

Now this match is, of course, a mecca for football fans. It's like Walsall against Port Vale – something you have just got to see.

I asked the people on Radio Clyde if there was any chance of a ticket, expecting them to say, 'Oh, the last one was sold about four years ago.'

But, just by chance, they did have a spare press pass.

I couldn't believe my luck.

'You mean, it's in the seats and everything?'

'Well, no,' they said. 'It's a standing place. Just behind the goal.'

That didn't sound so good.

'Aren't they a bit nationalistic in Glasgow?' I asked.

'No,' they said. 'Just keep your trap shut. No one will know.'

So off I went – a bit nervously, I must admit.

Of course, there is an incredible atmosphere at the stadium and the place is absolutely jammed pack solid. You can't move and the backs of your legs are getting soaking wet. Luckily, it's a reciprocal arrangement all the way down – which is fine for everyone except the blokes in the front who get it in the neck.

So I'm standing there minding my own business when this little bloke in front of me turns around and says, 'Hey, you!'

'Hmm?'

'Wha' sa' teem?'

Oh no, I'm thinking – how the hell do I get out of this?

'Och aye,' I say.

'What did you say?'

'It's a broa' brich' moonlich' nicht!'

'Are ye trying to be funny?'

'Och the noo,' I said, shaking my head vigorously.

'Wha' sa' teem?' he says.

'I don't know,' I say, 'I'm afraid I haven't got a programme.'

There was a stunned silence around me for a moment. Then it was all round the stadium:

'It's a sassenach, it's a sassenach, it's a . . .'

So the bloke looks me in the eye and says something like. 'Are ye tryin' tae be funny wi' me, pal? Ye came here and tryin' to be funny, yer sassa, an' I'll getta held o' yer heed and git yer and put it reet up yer ass. *I'm talkin' to you, Jimmy.*'

'Now I'll gi' yer one more chance an' if ye dinna tell me I'll put a foot in yer heed and kick ye up the. . . . WHA' SA' TEEEEEM!!!

Then I noticed he was pointing at his wrist.

Luckily I had a watch on.

'Ten to three,' I said.

I had turned puce green by now, but, by a miracle, I was standing at the Celtic end so I was all right.

10 Carrott Gets Saudi

The Abu Dhabi Curry Club

I arrived at Abu Dhabi airport at about two o'clock in the morning and within minutes of flying in, the expatriot Brits who were there to greet me had told me all I needed to know about the place. They seemed very keen to show me round and to give me all the gory details about people being stoned to death for adultery and hands being chopped off for nicking.

For heaven's sake, they said, don't ever drive into a car with only three numbers on the number plate – that means that it belongs to a member of the ruling family and you're in dire trouble if you do that.

And you are most definitely not supposed to drink and drive. In fact, you're not allowed to drink at all so, even if you get a taxi back to the hotel, you haven't clobbered the system – as often as not, the taxi driver drives you straight round to the police station. While they charge you for being drunk, he picks up his reward for bringing you in.

Although I'd been told that there was absolutely no smoking and drinking in Abu Dhabi, I don't think I've ever seen so many legless nicotine addicts as I did there. Everywhere you go, you find fags and booze. There's no escaping it.

In fact a lot of what I'd heard about the place turned out to be not entirely accurate. For example, everyone told me that it was going to be extremely hot and dry but, when I arrived, everything was covered in water. They had just had a fortnight of monsoon and for days it absolutely tipped down. I thought the first thing I'd have to buy was going to be a snorkel.

Abu Dhabi itself is about the size of Plymouth and, when you first see it, you wonder whether they are building it up or pulling it down – everything seems to be half completed or half demolished. There's untold amounts of money there, of course, and they are using a lot of it on the town itself so that, with all that building, it looks like a Lego town.

It is, in fact, quite easy to get into trouble out there. The ruling families run things in a completely autocratic way and, if you are not of Arab descent and reasonably wealthy, the law is very strict and life can be quite hairy.

For example, if you are involved in any accident, you are not allowed to move away until the police come to take names and details. Even if you've just bumped into someone's bumper or scraped a wing, you have to wait for the police. You can't even have your car repaired in Abu Dhabi without a chit from the police – and if you drive round the town with a car that is in disrepair, you're also in trouble.

On the other hand, members of the ruling families can get away with anything. If one of the sheik's relatives careered into the back of your car at 70 m.p.h. while you were waiting at a roundabout, there would be no two ways about it – you'd be guilty.

It would be a case of 'Why were you there just then? Did you give a hand signal? Did you have the right amount of petrol in your car? And did you try and take evasive action by driving on to the roundabout as you saw the other car approaching behind at 70 m.p.h.?'

The sheiks' seven or eight-year-old sons are allowed to own £25,000 cars and they hurtle up and down the main road to the airport in these gleaming Maseratis and Ferraris at about 130 m.p.h.

Woe betide anyone who gets in their way.

Occasionally one would be overtaken at 130 m.p.h. by an eight-year-old Saudi sheik in a Maserati, standing up to see over the steering-wheel, licking an ice-cream.

While I was in Abu Dhabi, I was invited to the BP Curry Club. This was a club that was set up by a group of Brits who really missed the curries they used to get back home. So they set up a club that would visit all the oddball little Indian restaurants in Abu Dhabi – they are usually to be found in rickety tin huts, and cater for the resident Indian manual labour.

Apparently the members had experienced some quite interesting meals – no one had actually died yet, although one or two had come quite close to it on occasions.

The meal I had was, I'm glad to say, in the Abu Dhabi Club itself. All the same, the curry was quite warm, to say the least. But they were very good about this at the club and always used to keep the bog rolls in the fridge.

One of the blokes at the Curry Club told me that something I should look out for while I was in Abu Dhabi was the holes. And it was true – with all that building work going on, I noticed there were big construction holes everywhere you looked.

What was interesting was that the labourers, who were for the most part from India and Bangladesh, used to do nothing for long periods of time except stand around peering into these holes.

Most odd, I thought. What a waste of time, how stupid can you get? But then you get into the habit of it. When you're walking by a hole, you've got to have a look into it. Then you see there's nothing in it except earth, so you stand for a while staring in and trying to find out what everyone else is looking at. Eventually you realize you've been peering into a bloody hole in the ground for about an hour – and you're certainly not going to move now in case something does happen.

I found that the only time people move away from the hole is when something *really* interesting happens – when there's an accident of any kind, or someone's scraped a wing of a car with their bicycle. So while the participants in the accident stand around and wait for the police to arrive, people drift away from their holes to stand around and inspect the scratch.

By the time the police arrive, there are just hundreds of people standing around, staring at the car driver, or the man on the bike, or the scratch. When the police have taken names and made notes everyone wanders off back to the holes.

Now and then you'd come across what was clearly a most favourable hole. That was one where there was something interesting lying in it – a rusty shovel, something like that. In fact outside the Holiday Inn where I was staying there was a really super hole. It had a dead dog in it. It was amazing that it hadn't been eaten but there it was – a dead dog in a hole.

The trouble was that you couldn't just walk in and look at it – you had to wait your turn. You had to queue for that one.

The rub of the brown

I was fast asleep in my hotel on the first night of my stay in Dubai when I was awoken by the most unearthly noise I think I have ever heard. At first I thought there was some riot going on – dervishes, bloodshed, something untoward and catastrophic.

What could it be? Had they televized to the Arab public the first episode of 'The Borgias'. No – that would have sent them to sleep.

I looked at my watch and saw that it was only twenty past five – I'd been asleep just two hours.

Then I realized that this shreaking and wailing was coming from loudspeakers. Within the space of minutes, thousands of Arabs appeared scurrying on to the rooftops of houses and shops, all kneeling down on little mats – in my direction!

What a welcome, I thought, this town obviously goes for comedy in a big way.

They were, of course, praying. It struck me that the Methodists should have thought of this ruse to get the faithful steamed up in, say, Guildford. If I could get a concession on raffia mats, I might suggest it to them.

I'm glad to say that I didn't have to spend too

much time in my hotel. Apart from anything else, the programmes they had on offer hardly recommended themselves. Dubai TV consists of the worst and the blandest of American-made programmes – when you consider that the British network get the best of American TV, boy does the worst keep you out of your hotel room.

Because of Arab morality, most of the shows were about Mom and Pop who were having a little problem with Mabellene because she wanted to stay out to ten o'clock to go to the disco with Bob who was a computer programmer – and that was the dramatic high point.

What made it worse was that the whole screen was obliterated by Arabic sub-titles, not placed at the bottom but shown full screen.

There was an additional problem in that you'd be watching this gripping saga when there would suddenly be a break of about three minutes while nothing appeared on the screen. After a while, you worked out that the films had been video'd from some illegal source and no one had bothered to edit the commercials out of the tape so they just blanked them out at the TV studio.

Before I had discovered this, I had given the hotel reception a hard time. When the blank screen first appeared, I phoned down to see if they could send up an engineer to put the telly right.

A little Indian electrician came up pretty quickly but, by the time he had arrived, the programme had returned.

He didn't speak English too well and my knowledge of Hindustani is limited to mutton vindaloo and two poppadoms, please.

'The screen has gone blank,' I said. 'Blank. As in,

er . . . Blankety. You know 'Blankety Blank'? Terry Wogan?'

'Terry Wogan,' he repeated, with a glint of recognition in his eye. He twirled a shiny screwdriver and produced a roll of black tape – every electrician in the world has a roll of black tape. As he twirled, he muttered a few words. I thought I heard an 'onion bhagi' in there but I was probably mistaken.

'Terry Logan,' he kept murmuring.

It happened again about twenty minutes later. So I called reception to ask for the engineer. This time it would be a great help, I said, if they pointed out to him what was wrong with the TV.

'Oh, he knows what's wrong with the TV,' they said. 'It's got a faulty Terry Wogan.'

I played some golf both in Dubai and Abu Dhabi and could never quite get used to the difference between Arab and English courses.

For a start, there is no grass and the whole course is sand – or at least the only grass that there is is in the bunkers. The greens are, of course, not called greens at all but 'browns' since they are made up of a sand and oil mix which gives a surprisingly good putting surface. It takes a bit of time to get used to the golfing terms they use because it all has to fit in with the lack of grass – so they talk about the 'rub of the brown' and 'through the brown'.

Another thing you don't often see at Gleneagles is golfers carrying their own grass with them. What happens in Abu Dhabi and Dubai is that you drive off the tee and set out, carrying with you a piece of plastic grass. If the ball lands on the fairway, you walk up to it, put your plastic grass down, plonk your ball on it and try to go for the next brown.

I got quite used to going around with my piece of grass, although on one or two occasions I found I could hit the grass further than the ball.

If you are unlucky enough to miss the fairway, which is designated by wooden posts, then you have to play the ball as it lies. In other words, it's just like playing out of a ten square mile bunker.

They also have very useful caddies out there. Quite often they manage to find your ball for you and, by the time you reach it, it is miraculously sitting up on a little heap of sand. Apparently the caddies think they are helping you out in this way and that you'll give them more money as a result.

There are unfortunately one or two hazards in playing golf Arab-style. There was an occasion when the club captain at Abu Dhabi arrived one morning to find several bulldozers in the middle of his eight-een-hole golf course. The land belonged to a sheik who had decided to build a race track for his horses across the eighth, ninth, thirteenth, fifteenth and seventeenth holes. So his men set up this race track, complete with grass and sprinkler system. Since it's exclusively for horses not golfers, the sheik gets very angry if anyone from the golf course strays on to his grass.

It's probably the only golf course in the world where the only strip of grass is strictly and officially out of bounds.

My host in Dubai was a guy called Julian Peck. Julian ran the Dubai Country Club and looked after us superbly well. One of those people who tend to be rather apprehensive and anxious to foresee any disaster, he was very concerned I didn't say anything on stage about sex, religion, politics or Arabs. So I assured him before I went on that I understood all about good taste and consideration for others.

Then I started my act by saying something like, 'There was this terrorist rabbi in a fez who was sexually assaulting a Roman Catholic camel when. . . .'

I was looking at Julian as I spoke. He was standing perfectly still staring at his watch, with an obvious malfunction of his wind-pipe going on.

I can be a real creep at times.

11 Sweet and Sour Labrador

Sweet and Sour Labrador

If you have a vague tendency towards claustrophobia and fear of crowds, then shopping in Birmingham's Bull Ring is probably best avoided. But this feverish Brummie imitation of a sardine tin is nothing compared to, say, three a.m. on a Sunday morning in Hong Kong.

It's a town that never stops – twenty-four hours a day, it simply pulsates with people. When you first go shopping there, it's a question of proffering apologies as you bump, push, barge and even strangle your way around the local trading arcades.

After a while you get fed up sounding like a bad comedy sketch – apologizing to everybody. So then you get into the way of the locals and even if you've just blinded someone with the tip of your umbrella, you merely look as inscrutable as the rest of them.

I'd always wanted to go to Hong Kong ever since I heard someone say on the Parkinson show that one of his favourite vices was buying an overcoat there at midnight. Now I know what he means – there's something rather debauched, even illicit about it.

Day or night, you can buy anything you want in Hong Kong – and, if you're Chinese, you can eat it. I discovered that the Chinese can apparently eat any-thing. Car parts, calculators, bedsteads – just wok it into some sauce and shove it down your throat. It's as simple as that.

The driving is fairly straightforward as well. They have two speeds in Hong Kong – 100 m.p.h. and stop. There are no hand signals because anyone foolish enough to put out his hand would be likely to see it disappearing into the distance attached to a wing mirror.

Indicators are occasionally used but only to fool other drivers. For instance, if you want to turn right, you indicate left. The car behind you will pull out to save time going round you. When he's on your outside accelerate! Now he'll force the traffic coming in the opposite direction to stop, if he's lucky, so the cars that would never have stopped to let you turn right are now brought to a grinding halt. See what I mean?

It's a road hog's paradise, Hong Kong – survival of the fastest. And I enjoyed every minute of it.

Just imagine it for yourself. No rules, no courtesy to other drivers – you just see a gap and head for it, regardless. It's 'First there gets there' and if you get a scrape on the way, what the hell! Everyone's driving cars from a Steve McQueen movie anyway – another gash in the roof won't hurt. Elbow on the horn, two fingers in the air, bum out of the window, who cares? Wonderful!

Not surprisingly, there's a great deal of carnage on the road and you see 'Drive Carefully' signs every-where you go. Unfortunately no driver can read them – take your eyes off the road for one moment in Hong Kong and you can end up well and truly in the wok.

I suppose that explains why Hong Kong TV is so full of public warning adverts. These are not exactly subtle. The one I remember best showed a man driving a car down a one-way street. Coming towards him from the other direction is another car. Cut to two women pedestrians, hands over their mouths in horror. They both drop their baskets and pedestrians are shown trampling through broken eggs that have spilt on to the pavement. The sound of two cars colliding. Cut to driver slumped over car with blaring horn. He is headless. Cut to other driver who is hopping up and down pointing to bent bumper with a samurai sword, dripping blood, in his hand.

Get the message?

The Chinese also have a passion for spitting. It's something they have done quite happily for centuries and no colonialists are going to stop them now. This obviously incenses the powers that be because, alongside the 'Drive Carefully' ads on television, there are anti-spitting warnings.

The only difference is that the ads advising people to be responsible on the road, keep the weekly death toll within three figures and so on, last some thirty seconds while the 'No Spitting' warnings last about two minutes.

It's then that you realize that the penalties for public gobbing in Hong Kong are far higher than those incurred by mowing down the local population.

No matter – people still spit and drivers still kill.

The one aspect of all this that did get to me was the incredibly high level of monoxide caused by all this manic, intense traffic. As one who pushes a Flymo round the lawn at home wearing a World War II gas mask, I was quite understandably paranoid.

That was why, when I first got there, I would drive even faster than the locals – I was desperate to get out of the smog and into my air-conditioned hotel room. When I realized that the system in the hotel actually drew in air from the outside to re-circulate inside, I hit the Valium.

One of the most important discoveries I made during my trip was the true definition of a milli-second. It's the time between the moment traffic lights in Hong Kong turn from red to amber and the driver behind blares his horn. I'll remember that.

One of the things I was particularly looking forward to in my stay in Hong Kong was the food. Now, I'm quite partial to the occasional chow mein – in fact, we always keep the menu from our local takeaway – called The Shirley Temple, would you believe – so that now and then we can order a Cantonese mêlée, Peking Duck or whatever. In fact, we actually play bingo in our house using the Shirley Temple menu. We were fed up with the '88 Two Fat Ladies' bit, so now we shout out, 'Egg Foo Yung Special with water chestnuts and sweet corn No 12'.

We got this idea from a football gag that was doing the rounds some years ago. Wolverhampton Wanderers had just appointed a new manager, a very nice man called Sammy Chung. After one of his first games as manager, a Wolves supporter walked up to him and said, 'I loike yer number noine, our kid.'

'Oh, John Richards,' said Sammy.

'Nah,' said the bloke. 'That sweet and sour chicken with the soy sauce.'

So, back in Hong Kong, my mouth watered at the thought of all those Cantonese restaurants awaiting my arrival. Little did I know what I was in for.

Our first evening in Hong Kong we were invited out to dinner by the promoters. We were about to experience, they said, a true, authentic Chinese meal in genuine ethnic surroundings.

At about eight o'clock, we were collected from our hotel and taken to an area called Kennedy Town – it's Hong Kong's answer to the Black Hole of Calcutta.

As usual, the streets were packed with people. We had a particularly good taxi driver who scored twenty bonus points by running three red lights and scaring the wits out of a nun. When we arrived in Kennedy Town, he indicated right, turned left and let us out of the car – badly shaken but still alive.

Besides the promoters, there were four of us there and it quickly became clear that we were the only Europeans within several square miles. All around the Chinese were staring at us. Was it with menace? Hilarity? Disbelief? It was impossible to tell – they are all just so damned inscrutable!

My manager John Starkey was convinced that they thought we were doolally but it seemed to me that they assumed we were looking for a quick way out of life.

Then we saw the 'genuine ethnic surroundings'. The restaurant consisted of several sheets of plastic strung over some metal tubes. A dozen or so fluorescent lights hung precariously at bizarre angles from the ceiling. It was like a very cheap disco that has been set up in a bivouac.

All this was set up in the gutter. The customers

actually sat in a clear area on the pavement where some rickety tables awaited us.

Under the low, inflammable plastic roof, a couple of Chinese chefs were working their earlobes off over two roaring gas-fed furnaces. We watched them for a while and were most impressed by their dexterity as they chopped the food into woks and tossed it around, keeping several meals going at the same time and dishing them all out at amazing speed.

I asked for the toilet and they just laughed.

So we sat down at one of the tables which was positioned between a tank full of fish and a basket containing some noisy and very much alive chickens.

One of the promoters knew about four words of Cantonese, one of which was 'wicky'. I was never quite sure what 'wicky' meant and nor, it turned out, was he. All he knew was that if you shouted 'wicky, wicky' furiously enough, things would happen. So, whenever he wanted anything during the evening, he would hold up certain fingers, give the magic word, and all hell would break loose.

The first thing they brought along were some chopsticks and a pot of scalding hot tea. As this arrived, our host waved away the cups and plunged all the chopsticks into the teapot. He had to sterilize them, he said – you never could tell in Kennedy Town.

One of our party that night was Joe Dolce, who had just had a hit single 'Shaddupayaface'. I had expected him to be a fifty-year-old Italian immigrant from Australia but, in fact, Joe is about thirty and from California.

Like most Californians, he is heavily into nature, ecology, saving the ant – that sort of thing – and he was, at first, very excited at the prospect of experiencing genuine Cantonese fare. However he was most concerned as to whether there was enough fibre in the food.

'Where's the fibre, man?' was one of his first questions. 'Do you leave the fibre in the food?'

'Wicky wicky,' went the maître d'.

'The food's full of fibre,' said Joe, fully satisfied.

'Fine, fine,' I said. 'Thank goodness for that. I couldn't eat it if the fibre was missing. I'm into muesli myself.'

At this point, the maître d' proudly showed us the food that was on offer. There were dozens of bowls containing meat-like substances that looked distinctly dubious. I dreaded to think what was in them.

'What's in the bowls?' I asked nervously.

That started it. The maître d' failed to understand us so several minutes following during which we all made animal noises at him – flapping our arms, quacking like ducks, grunting like pigs. He didn't seem to recognize any of them.

For a laugh, I did my elephant impression, trumpeting and waving my right arm from my head.

His face lit up.

'Wicky wicky,' he cried, leaping about, piling huge amounts of meat into a wok.

'Oh, come on!' I said. 'He can't be serious.'

'It's all right,' said Joe. 'He's telling you it's full of fibre.'

He looked at his plate.

'Hey, man, do these look like ants to you?'

By this time, John had turned the colour of some of the meat dishes and I wasn't feeling too good myself. But we had a couple of beers and they brought us some vegetable stuff to start the meal. It was bland, but at least it didn't taste too dangerous.

148

Then they asked me to choose my next course – from the fish tank. I had had a fair idea of what was going to happen so, while I was eating the first course, I had been looking out for a fish without too much fungus on it. I had spotted one that looked a little like the editor of the *Sun* so I thought 'I'll have 'im.'

When I pointed him out, one of the Cantonese standing by whipped the fish out of the tank with a bit of netting and flung him into the air. It landed in the gutter and a coolie, who up until now had been peeling onions in a corner, rushed over with a big wooden club, battered this fish around the head and slit its gullet so that its insides toppled out on to the ground. By the time he'd stuck four needles through it and steamed it in front of us, I'd just gone right off the idea.

Anyway they served the fish up with various other odd things that I definitely didn't want to know too much about.

It tasted awful.

But then things began to improve. They brought us some hot food and I got some chicken – I'm fairly sure it was chicken – and some sauce and vegetables. It was delicious and I was beginning to enjoy my meal when I spotted the coolie who had been doing the whirling dervish act with the fish working very carefully around the chicken basket.

What he was doing was reaching into the basket, which had a small hole in the top, pulling a chicken out, bending its neck and very calmly slitting its throat. Of course, blood was spurting everywhere as he threw the chicken, bleeding but still alive, into a big open basket. So in another corner was now a pile of chickens dying extremely noisily – the sound they

149

made reminded me of the call to prayer in Abu Dhabi.

By the time he got to the sixth chicken, I was really beginning to feel decidedly ill with all this blood everywhere and these death-throe noises all around. But then he actually picked up a chicken, slit its throat, threw it towards the basket – and missed. This mortally wounded chicken, blood spurting everywhere, ran off down the road squawking with a new-found sense of freedom, hotly pursued by the coolies from the restaurant.

The chicken disappeared under a large lorry. First of all the coolies tried poking at it with large sticks. Then they had a go at soft-talking it out – not very successfully since the Chinese are physically incapable of soft-talking. Anything they say, whatever the circumstances, sounds like an order to jump into an open grave and to cover yourself with cement. The chicken obviously thought so too.

One of the coolies had a bright idea and ran off at high speed. He came back a few moments later carrying, would you believe, a handful of corn, which he proceeded to throw under the lorry. He clearly believed that the chicken – blood spurting every-where, staring death in the face – would be taken in by a bit of corn!

Finally they decided to release the handbrake on the lorry and pushed it back, to reveal the chicken waving a white handkerchief.

Feebly protesting, it was taken back to join the unfortunate birds noisily awaiting the last rites. They were not long in coming. Out came a couple of coolies carrying a large vat of boiling water; in went the chickens – silence – out came the chickens, to be swiftly plucked and gutted before our very eyes.

It was really a question of who would throw up first. Joe Dolce won.

'I think there's too much fibre in the food, man. Maybe we should have ordered the muesli, after all.'

Looking at the food on the table, it was a case of 'Are you going to eat that – or have you?'

To cap it all, it was just at that moment that a dog came prancing down the street. Now, since this was the Year of the Dog, the Chinese, who are very superstitious, had thought it best to leave dogs off the menu for twelve months – just to play safe. Unfortunately I wasn't aware of this embargo and I panicked.

'Don't point at the dog,' I screamed. 'Ignore it. The last thing I want is sweet and sour labrador!'

While I was in Hong Kong I heard the drummer Bev Bevan had had to drop out of a European tour he was on with ELO because he was very ill with a stone in his kidneys. I got the message that he was in hospital and that, rather than operate, they wanted first of all to see whether he could pass the stone away.

He was going to be in hospital for at least a week and was in great pain, so I wanted to get a telegram to him to cheer him up a bit. This proved to be something of a problem.

I wanted to send him a cable that was appropriate to the occasion, rather than a boring 'Get well soon, chin up' message, and decided to send the following:

'GLEETINGS FLOM HONG KLONG O MIGHTY SKLIN BLASHER. I HEAR YOU STONED AGAIN. HA HA OLD CLANTONESE YOKE. GET WELL SOON BIG BUDDY AND ROCK ON. NO ON SECOND THOUGHTS ROCK OUT.'

It was obviously important that I send the message with the right spelling for maximum effect. As I took it to the hotel receptionist, I was a little apprehensive that she might think that I was taking the mick out of the way she spoke.

In fact, there was no problem – until the hotel manager, who had been told that I was an international, universal megastar, insisted on helping out.

'Ah now, Mister Carrott. Is a good job I came because I can see that she has spelt message wrong. The silly girl has spelt gleetings with a "leh". No "leh" in gleetings, yes?'

'Well, no . . . not normally but this is, er, . . . this is the way we spell greetings in Birmingham. It's the Birmingham spelling – where we come we spell greetings with, er, with a "leh".'

'Ah! Is same with flom?'

'Yes.'

Then he spotted something else on the telegram.

'But silly girl definitely wrong here, Mister Carrott. HONG KLONG. No "leh" in Klong, eh? They no say Klong in Birmingham, yes?'

'You're right there, Charlie Chan,' I muttered, thinking fast.

'Look, this friend of mine, you see, has a lisp. You understand "Lisp"?'

'Lisp?' He looked puzzled.

'Yeth, lithp. As in thwetty thockth. Thuper thonic. Thilly thod.'

'A lisp,' he said. 'I understand "lisp".'

He turned to his receptionist and garbled at her in Chinese – obviously he was explaining that Mr Carrott had a lisp which accounted for the 'leh' in 'gleetings' flom Hong Klong.

'She now understands, Mr Carrott. Have a nice day.'

And, with that, he walked off.

The receptionist smiled pityingly at me as she wiped her face dry.

'Now,' she said. 'Ith that with a "leh" or without, ath the manager thaid?'

I thought, 'I don't believe this – a Chinese receptionist with a lisp?'

So we spent the next ten minutes lisping at each other. I got my 'leh' in in the gleetings teleglam and the mighty sklin-basher got the message.

He also got his rock out.

Unexploded gases

Did you know you can set light to a fart? It's an amazing fact when you first hear it, isn't it?

I got into this a few years ago. I was at a party and this bloke I was talking to says, 'Eh, Jasper, there's Harry. He sets light to his farts, you know.'

'You what?' I exclaimed. 'He sets light to his what?'

'His farts. He sets light to his farts. It's the methane gas or something. Apparently he's quite a dab hand at it.'

Several people who couldn't help hearing this revelation joined the conversation.

'Impossible!'

'Don't talk through your arse!'

But this bloke was adamant that it could be done. He had actually witnessed this particular form of arson about. He said that you might not be able to declaim Shakespeare through that orifice but you could certainly imitate a blow lamp. He went over to fetch Harry so that he could demonstrate his art.

Harry was most indignant that anyone had questioned his ability and, without more ado, he dropped his pants. Out with the Swan Vestas and BRRUMMPHHH!

Quite astonishing. We were all very impressed.

I set out forthwith to learn the art of lighting farts. I stoked up on flatulent foods: curries worked very well, so did beans and sardines. Yes, sardines – remarkable what you discover in the course of scientific research, isn't it?

But it's not as easy as it looks and after several tries I gave up. I discovered that it was all a question of timing – you've got to get the timing right somehow. Match to fart, fart to match – very difficult.

Positioning is very important as well. Apparently a course in yoga can do wonders.

The main reason that I gave it up was that I discovered that it could be highly dangerous – so be warned!

This was brought home to me at a party a few weeks after Harry's revelation to us all.

Harry was there, of course. He had gained some notoriety in the neighbourhood for his exploits. In fact, he was becoming a bit of a pain about it all. At the merest indication of doubt at his prowess, he would proudly BRRUUMMPHH without warning and seemingly at will.

As I arrived at the party, there was Harry up to his normal tricks. This time he was busily trying to impress a couple of young ladies with his art.

Unfortunately on this occasion, he tried to impress a little too much and had what could best be described as a blowback.

One can only imagine the pain. He was a big,

hairy bugger as well. He let out a blood-curdling scream and writhed around on the floor.

I just managed to stop someone releasing the fire extinguisher all over him and suggested that we had better get him to hospital pretty quickly.

Harry was in such agony that he certainly couldn't sit down in the back of a car. So we found someone with a station wagon and bundled him into the back of it – with his bum stuck out of the window.

Well, I thought, it would cool it off if nothing else.

So here was this station wagon, hairing off towards the hospital, with four blokes inside it in hysterics and a big singed bum sticking out of the side.

We got some funny looks.

Now you either know about the fart phenomenon or you don't. As luck wouldn't have it, we got stopped by a copper who didn't. It was only to be expected, I suppose – you don't see a big singed bum travelling at 70 m.p.h. every day of the week.

'Evening sir,' he said to me. 'What we got here? Bit of moonin' goin' on by the looks of it.'

'No, no, it's Harry. He's set light to his fart.'

'He set light to his what?' said the copper, reaching into his side carrier for a bag to blow into.

'His fart! It's his party trick. He'd show you but he wouldn't be on top form right now.'

But he was still suspicious and he reached for his walkie-talkie.

'Hello, sarge. Perkins 'ere. Look, sarge, I know it's a bit late but, well, can you tell me, I mean – can you set light to a fart?'

Silence.

'A fart, yes?'

Silence.

'No, I haven't been drinking!'

157

Silence.

'Well, I've never heard of it either but the thing is there's a bloke done 'is bum in with one 'ere.'

We finally arrived at the hospital, escorted by the copper who was by now fascinated to find out the results of such an exercise. The four of us each took a limb and carried Harry into the casualty ward. We were particularly careful not to let his bum scrape along the ground.

We had settled down a bit by now and were beginning to feel a bit of sympathy for the poor bugger.

'Shame, Harry. It was a bloomin' good one, mind. The daffodils never stood a chance.'

At that point an extremely large, important-looking woman appeared. It was the matron – five foot ten of stiff white starch.

'What's all this commotion?' she asked, very plum in mouth.

Whehey! We drew lots for who was going to have the pleasure of telling her.

She looked at Harry, then at us and, in her best Oxford English, exclaimed, 'Has he set light to his farts?'

Mystical musings of a contented till

or I £CHING!

I've never really understood
why people who
write poetry like
this
get paid a
bob
or two
surely it's not difficult to write
it
in fact I just have
haven't I
oh no
you must put lots
of words in

like
memory
tomorrow misty
nebulous
ethereal that's a good one
phew, it's ever such hard work
honest
right then
now
where's my
money?